LEADING
THE WAY

STEVE LETARTE
As Told To
NATE RYAN

PAGE PUBLISHING, INC.
New York, NY

First originally published by Page Publishing, Inc. 2018

ISBN 978-1-64298-386-9 (Paperback)
ISBN 978-1-64298-387-6 (Hardcover)
ISBN 978-1-64298-388-3 (Digital)

Printed in the United States of America

FOREWORD

How our paths eventually crossed is a long story. The fact that they did was a game changer for us both.

Steve's approach to our future together was simple and easy to embrace. We would only succeed by working closely together, and we would become great friends while building that mutual trust.

Steve helped me understand how to be a team player. He showed me the importance of being available and accountable.

Steve possesses all the qualities of a successful leader with a unique ability to rally his team into believing in their own success.

This book is a special look at his life, both personally and professionally, that I think will enlighten and educate.

Dale Earnhardt Jr.

CHAPTER 1

I Need Your Help

AFTER FIFTEEN YEARS AT HENDRICK Motorsports ... five seasons and ten wins as Jeff Gordon's crew chief ... countless miles and hours on airplanes ... who knew that November 23, 2010, a wet and dreary Tuesday, would be the biggest day of my career?

It was the day that changed the course of my life forever.

And yet as I walked out of a conference room, I surely thought I was getting fired.

The 2010 Sprint Cup season was among the worst of Gordon's career, and certainly the worst during my tenure as his crew chief.

After five years together, we didn't win once in thirty-six starts, and we finished in the top ten seventeen times—almost half as many as the record thirty top tens we had achieved only three years earlier. We had tried fishing trips, sports psychologists, and other well-intentioned attempts at team-building, but nothing was working anymore despite our best efforts.

For the second time in three seasons, the NASCAR superstar had gone winless, and it was my fault. On the Tuesday after the season finale at Homestead-Miami Speedway (where we placed thirty-seventh, the second time in three races we had matched our worst finish of the season), I sat mentally exhausted in a mammoth boardroom at Hendrick Motorsports. As general manager Doug Duchardt debriefed with crew chiefs and about a dozen Hendrick executives over what had been a mostly disappointing season (six wins, all by Jimmie Johnson on the way to a fifth championship), I stared out a window and daydreamed about a long, miserable year.

I'd had enough, so much so that I barely noticed the oddity of our boss, Rick Hendrick, entering halfway through the meeting.

When it was over, I popped up, ready to beeline for the door, when Rick said in one of his familiar authoritative tones, "Hey, Stevie, I need to see you for a minute," and motioned me toward team president Marshall Carlson's office.

A moment of clarity struck while I was gathering my things at the enormous conference table.

What race teams would have openings for next season? Who is most likely to be hiring?

There was no way the best team in NASCAR could keep me employed. By the time I'd walked past the two dozen chairs to the door leading to Marshall's office, I already was resigned to my fate. I wouldn't blame Rick Hendrick for wanting to cut me loose. There'd be no argument here. I'd do the same thing in his position.

Rick, Marshall, and I sat at a smaller round table inside Marshall's office, further confirming my fears. We were team owner, president, and underperforming head coach meeting after a disappointing review of the season.

This is the way terminations happen in professional sports.

Except this one.

"Stevie," Rick said, "I need you to do me a favor. If Dale Jr. is unsuccessful in my cars, it'll be a black eye on me and a black eye on this company that I'll never live down. I need your help."

In context, this was one of the most extraordinarily positioned job offers in NASCAR history.

Beyond being the most successful team owner in NASCAR history with eleven Cup championships, Rick Hendrick also is a billionaire whose automotive empire encompasses nearly one hundred dealerships stretching from coast to coast.

I'm a small-town racer's son from Maine who moved to North Carolina as a sophomore in high school without any NASCAR career ambitions before Rick Hendrick gave me a job sweeping floors. I didn't attend college. I wasn't a prize prodigy out of MIT.

But that was how I was being treated by the most powerful man I'd ever work for, as if I were the most highly coveted commodity in the room.

At the time, though, it completely was lost on me. My head was spinning.

In the span of ten minutes, my mind had wandered from being gainfully employed to out of work after fifteen years with one team, to mentally blanketing the greater Charlotte area with mass mailings of my résumé.

There were no words as I tried to regain my bearings, so Rick began filling the silence left by my dazed state.

He removed an index card from his shirt and began writing numbers.

Large numbers.

"I'm going to pay this extra if you can win a race," Rick said. "This much extra if you can make the Chase." This was NASCAR's version of the playoffs.

"These will replace his current bonus, right?" asked Marshall, who was in charge of making the team's budget work.

"No, this is in addition to it," Rick replied.

Marshall's face turned a little pale.

I still hadn't said a word, but it began to sink in that my situation rapidly was improving, even though I hadn't processed the bonuses yet.

There were no incentives or convincing necessary to take the job. The answer was obvious once the shock lifted.

"Well, yeah, boss," I told Mr. Hendrick. "I'm in. I'll do whatever you need me to do.

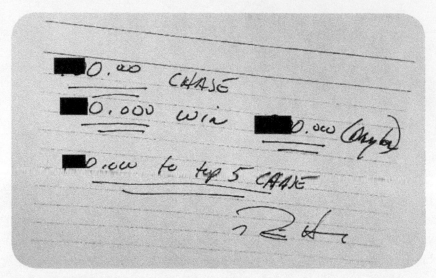

The index card on which Rick Hendrick drew up contract addendums to reflect my new position as crew chief of the No. 88 Chevrolet (yes, that really is Rick's signature). **Credit: Letarte Family Collection**

I would have agreed to the move solely out of my loyalty to Hendrick Motorsports, which single-handedly was responsible for putting me on the map in NASCAR.

But there was another reason too.

In life, the only constant is change, as difficult, painful, and unnerving as it may seem.

The most successful people in life are those who view change as an opportunity, in contrast to those who see it as a negative that can turn their worlds upside down.

It's impossible to insulate your life from the uncontrollable events that will shape it, which is why you must welcome those events as a gateway to personal growth.

I'd spent my entire working life at Hendrick Motorsports, but it wasn't a static existence by any means. I'd been promoted from floor sweeper to tire specialist to mechanic to car chief to crew chief.

I'd been an active participant as Jeff Gordon won races and remained a title contender through three crew chiefs and significant personnel shuffles. I'd watched firsthand as Hendrick built a team from scratch for Jimmie Johnson, who would win seven championships.

There were incessant examples of how results always improved after every major change at Hendrick Motorsports. The company's growth dovetailed with NASCAR's explosion through the 1990s and 2000s.

Ten years ago, I went to my first Daytona 500 as a crew chief with a Nokia flip phone that I thought was the coolest thing I ever owned. Today, I can order a gizmo off Amazon on an iPhone and have it on my doorstep the next morning.

You can change with the world or be left behind.

So I was all in on becoming the new crew chief of the most popular driver in NASCAR, who was fresh off the worst two seasons of his career.

* * * * *

Now it was time to tell the rest of the world—and quickly. Beyond myself, the only others in the know were those involved in the decision—Rick Hendrick, Marshall Carlson, Jeff Gordon, and Rick's two most trusted lieutenants, Doug Duchardt and Ken Howes.

Even Dale Earnhardt Jr. didn't know yet.

It wouldn't stay that way for long, though, so I needed to hustle back up the main road on the Hendrick campus to the shop shared by Jimmie Johnson and Jeff Gordon to tell my guys they had a new driver named Dale Earnhardt Jr.

But first, I needed to inform the most important person in my life. As I left the conference room, I grabbed my phone and called my wife, Tricia, while walking up the hill to my office.

"Hey, listen, we need to talk about something," I said, preparing to brace her for the news.

Understandably, she didn't grasp the gravity of the situation while in the 3:00 p.m. carpool line. And an already scheduled date night for the Letartes also loomed that evening as the perfect opportunity to delay an in-depth conversation.

"I've got to get the kids," she said. "We'll talk tonight."

"No! We need to talk now before you see this on *SportsCenter*!'"
Tricia began to cry. She thought I had been fired.

"No, wait! I didn't get fired. I'm going to crew-chief for Dale Jr."
She cried harder.

The reaction was partly about inheriting the pressure of working with NASCAR's most popular driver. But Tricia later would say it was mostly Dale's legendary reputation for partying off the track that scared her. She didn't want her husband and father of their two children out late at night with his new driver, a bachelor whose persona was beer drinking and hell raising.

Tricia also had listened to Dale Jr.'s contentious scanner dialogue during races with his previous crew chiefs. These were vulgarity-laden, mean-spirited conversations, and she worried that I was just another poor soul who would go down in flames if Dale didn't run well.

It also was about my relationship with Jeff Gordon. He might exist in a different social universe, and we didn't go to dinner regularly, but Jeff truly was a great friend. If we ever were in dire need, he'd be there.

I would entrust him with my kids, Tyler and Ashlyn, both of whom also began crying when Tricia broke the news.

"Ty, why are you crying?" Tricia asked.

My son said, "Well, I like Jeff. What if Dale doesn't like me?"

She told him, "Well, you know, Dale Jr. has a go-kart track." And he stopped crying.

That was enough to win my son over.

* * * * *

With my family secured, now it was time to win over the rest of my coworkers, starting with Chad Knaus, the crew chief who had guided Jimmie Johnson to five consecutive championships.

I've known Chad for more than twenty years. We met in the summer of 1995, when I was cleaning Jeff Gordon's shop and Chad was changing tires and working as a fabricator on the No. 24.

He has a drive and desire to be successful in his career unlike anyone I've ever met. He is one of the greatest crew chiefs of all time, and it was his ambition to achieve that goal since the moment he entered NASCAR.

Though it wasn't his driver changing crew chiefs, this would be a huge shift for Chad. For eight years, his team had worked side by side under the same roof as Jeff Gordon's team. Now Jeff, who had played a major role in brokering the deal to bring Jimmie Johnson and Knaus to Hendrick, would be leaving the building (because Hendrick organized its four cars into two-car shops, and this move would pair Dale Earnhardt Jr. and Jimmie Johnson).

We were telling a guy who had won five championships that his entire foundation was being flipped over, and Gordon, the guy who won four championships and co-owned the team, was headed to the shop next door and being replaced by a driver without a championship.

It was a lot for Chad to take in, but we hashed it out over thirty minutes and then gathered the Nos. 24 and 48 teams together. I stood in front of our eighty or so guys and told them Jeff Gordon was leaving all of them. There were some who had worked for Jeff longer than I had, but they opened their arms up to embrace Dale Jr., and a lot of it was a credit to Chad being a prime example. He had accepted a fundamental change—two days after winning his fifth championship.

My next meeting was with Jeff Gordon, and it might as well have been a trip back in time. We met in the same office at Jeff Gordon Inc. (on the second floor of the shop, just above where his cars were built). In the same place a little more than five years earlier, he had sat me down and said, "I want you to be my guy."

This was an entirely different conversation, but it was no less classy, professional, and uplifting. There wasn't a lot to say because I'd had a few hours to absorb the change. Rick had let me know it wasn't as if Jeff just wanted to switch crew chiefs. This was bigger than that, with a lot more layers to the decision.

In true Jeff Gordon fashion, Jeff spoke from the heart and said, "Listen, we're great friends, but this is going to be better for both of us." Truth be known, he was a four-time champion who went win-less the previous season and didn't deserve it, so something had to change. But he never would say that.

Instead, he took the Jeff Gordon approach of "I need something different. Jimmie and I are good friends, and the competition is start-ing to blur and strain our friendship. We're starting to butt heads, and we can't have that because we've all worked too hard for this to be successful." It was a case of two alpha males causing internal conflict, and he was headed over to the team's other two-car building because of that, not because of our struggles.

Jeff was a big-enough man that he could see the importance of keeping Jimmie successful after five straight championships and the significance to Hendrick of having Dale Earnhardt Jr. running well.

There were team elements of success, sponsorship, and strength that made it more than just about Jeff Gordon. He saw it from all these different angles in a way that other professional athletes of his stature never would.

He took a day out of his life just to fly to North Carolina (his family then lived in New York), sit down with me face-to-face, and say, "Hey, this isn't personal. Rick and I saw we needed to make a change." It was his way of not placing blame, which I appreci-ated. Because looking back now, he probably should have said, "It's because you're young and making a ton of mistakes."

In between all the meetings, a million phone calls and texts were pouring in from everybody who wanted to help advise me on how to handle my relationship with Dale.

I forcefully and politely turned them all away because I wanted to do this on my own. Much of the advice was from the same people who already were involved with Dale's team, and the results were clear.

With that in mind, my final step was to huddle with Dale's inner circle—Laura Scott, the No. 88 PR rep, and Mike Davis, his brand manager—to schedule a meeting about how I wanted to over-haul the approach to his calendar.

The bombshell news release announcing the changes, which also included moving Dale's current crew chief, Lance McGrew, to

Mark Martin's No. 5, went public late that afternoon, shortly before I left the shop at 6:00 p.m. It was all over the news on what typically was one of the NASCAR season's quietest weeks. Rick Hendrick had blown up his team two days after winning the championship and caught everyone completely off guard.

And among the most surprised was Dale Earnhardt Jr. At some point in my whirlwind afternoon, I'd seen the team's massive red helicopter (nicknamed Airwolf) land on the campus, and I knew that inside was Dale, who personally had been summoned by Rick Hendrick.

All the groundwork was laid for a successful transition. But none of it would matter without convincing the driver.

We needed total buy-in from Dale Earnhardt Jr.

And that was where I was headed next, once I had his cell number.

CHAPTER 11

Hey, I'm Dale

I KNEW NASCAR's MOST POPULAR driver well in passing from seeing him in the garage and at Hendrick debriefs and team events, but we hadn't talked on the phone, much less exchanged a text.

Not only did I not have Dale Earnhardt Jr.'s number, I also didn't have his address.

With one hand on the wheel of my Tahoe and the other clutching directions to Dale's sprawling two-hundred-acre estate, I fumbled my way to our initial meeting as crew chief and driver on the day after our pairing was announced.

My first impression of Dale's house was that it was enormous. That's what everyone sees. But that was not what struck me.

It was how much racing stuff was inside.

His two championship trophies from the Xfinity Series were given prominent display. His 2004 replica of the Harley J. Earl Trophy—given annually to the winner of the Daytona 500, NASCAR's biggest race—was sitting on a stone area by his fireplace.

If you were watching a Hollywood blockbuster on the massive flat screen in Dale Earnhardt Jr.'s house, you still would know his singular purpose in life was racing. I knew this was a guy I wanted to work with, because he wanted to look at his trophies while he was watching TV.

I'll admit it wasn't what I was expecting. Even I didn't have trophies all throughout my house. This guy had trophies in his living room. Racing was his entire life, not just a side job, as the conventional wisdom about Dale Jr. might have indicated.

It proved that NASCAR really mattered to him. He probably would have been a star regardless because of his last name, but this proved to me pretty quickly that he *really* cared about being a success too. That was pretty cool.

As awkward as it was getting to his place, the first lengthy conversation with Dale was nearly as stiff. We just talked to try to get that awkwardness out of the way of "I'm Steve. It's nice to meet you." "Hey, I'm Dale." We stood there in his kitchen and just tried to maintain the banter about anything and everything. A lot of it was just keeping words in the air.

It helped set the dynamics of our friendship. I talked a lot. Dale didn't. He liked hanging out with me because I filled the air, and silence was the enemy at this point. I would switch between topics that had no significance other than I needed him to talk. The point subtly was driven home that I needed words coming from his mouth as an active participant. I wouldn't be able to read him if he just stood there.

We talked mostly about life. This wasn't about hammering out the nuts and bolts for winning a championship. It was foundational. His dad was a seven-time NASCAR champion. My dad had been building stock cars since I was a kid. We were both racers' kids and had so much in common at these weird levels. We both grew up at racetracks, and we both loved what we did for a living.

But it felt a lot like a seventh-grade dance. It wasn't a fear of getting to know each other. Instead, there was a self-conscious anticipation of beginning something good together. It was two people who wanted this to be right so badly that no one dared say anything or do anything that could upset the other.

It felt very prim and proper—the opposite of what it would become a few years later, when I would sling the front door open and waltz into his house without even knocking (but maybe pausing to ask, "Hey, are you up? I'm getting a beer out of your bar.")

This was more like two people on their first date.

That formality had its positives. I appreciated the lack of "Well, I'm Dale Jr., and this is the way it should be." There was none of that. If you'd walked in on the meeting, you would have thought this was a driver trying to sign his first ever deal.

There was just an instant connection of how amazingly humble this guy was. It didn't fit with the stories that had circulated about him, that Dale Jr. didn't put the effort in to run better.

I'd worked my entire life for Hendrick Motorsports, the best team in NASCAR, and I wasn't going to have time for a guy that half-assed it. I just had worked for a driver who won ninety-two races and four championships. Jeff Gordon worked at it.

My office was adjacent to a crew chief whose team had won eighty-three races and seven titles. Chad Knaus works at it too. Hard.

My preconceived notions before becoming Dale Earnhardt Jr.'s crew chief were thus: *Why will I go out of my way to help him if he's not going to go out of his way to help himself? I'm busy, and I have a whole race team to manage. I'm not going to have the time for a driver who isn't a self-starter.*

Of course, I had those thoughts before we began working together. How could you not? His last name alone made him an icon whose every move had been deconstructed and dissected.

I buried all those opinions when I went to meet him for myself, and then I didn't get any of that attitude from him. It was like having a buddy tell you the food at a restaurant was awful. You get sent there for a company function and pleasantly discovered that everything was delicious and the service was terrific.

The Dale Jr. that I'd be working with wasn't an entitled and rigid malcontent unwilling to adapt to whatever path I laid out; instead, I received an unbelievably reciprocal commitment to becoming his crew chief.

He was in, even though he didn't have to be. He made it work, though at this point, it was more about just giving the change a chance to work.

After we'd gotten past the small talk, I laid out some of the plan for rebuilding his career. I ensured he knew the shop was happy to have him—and that included Chad Knaus and Jimmie Johnson—even though he had accomplished far less.

Since leaving Dale Earnhardt Inc., the team his late father built, in 2008 for Hendrick in one of the most anticipated driver moves in history, Dale mostly had struggled mightily in three seasons with the team.

Though he made the playoffs in 2008, Dale hadn't won in ninety-two starts when we entered our first season together. He finished twenty-fifth with a career-low two top fives in the 2009 points standings and twenty-first with three top fives in the 2010 points standings.

It had shattered his confidence, and he understandably was intimidated to join a shop whose culture was built on winning—not just posting good results, but winning!

Dale had one win in four seasons, but I told him the past wouldn't matter. We would solve his slump. I would be asking a lot of him, more than he ever had been asked to do before, but I told him that it would be worth it, particularly if he asked just as much out of me.

I nearly regurgitated the speech that Jeff Gordon had delivered to me when I'd become his crew chief five years earlier. I wasn't smart enough then to understand why Jeff told me, "Listen, this will only work if you treat me like everybody else on this race team." He would say that a hundred times in a row, but when you're twenty-six, as I was then, it's hard to do.

Jeff Gordon got the wrong end of my crew chief career. I was young and worked hard but didn't work smart and didn't have a good vision. I took all the learning blocks from my time with Jeff Gordon and laid it all out for Dale that this was how we could get better.

With the structure and organization that is necessary to establish the platform to make cars go fast, I knew the results would come.

Dale would benefit simply because I'd learned how to build successful teams during my seasons with Jeff, and I knew exactly what was needed on the new team.

But it started with getting him to believe. I told him that the best shop in NASCAR, the one he held in such high regard, was glad to have him without telling him "Hey, we're going to be winners"; it was "The winners are excited to have you." Connect the dots.

It was the day before Thanksgiving, so I wrapped up our conversation after a couple of hours with a final request. Dale was traveling the following Thursday morning to Las Vegas to accept his eighth straight Most Popular Driver Award.

"Hey, man, do you mind if I go with you?" I asked, hoping he wouldn't.

"No, not at all," he said.

It would be the first major step in my plan to spend as much time with him as possible, an integral part of our strategy to improve.

In my meeting with Rick Hendrick, I'd stressed that to fix things with Dale, we would need to be inseparable away from the racetrack. It was perhaps the biggest mistake I'd made with Jeff: I should have been more involved with him away from the car.

With Dale, I planned on getting to know him as well as I possibly could, and Hendrick had assured me that I would have its fleet of planes and helicopters at my disposal so that Dale and I could travel together to form a very strong bond. All those conversations away from the track would help build his faith in me and help ensure there never would be a point at which I questioned his desire.

I knew his struggles were much more complicated than just the race car. Jimmie Johnson wins all the time, but every car he drives isn't a winning car. *It's how the driver and team work together that determine success.*

When my first talk with Dale Jr. ended, I left with more questions than answers. But I also had a direction that was crystallized in a note to myself about the meeting: "This isn't a guy you get to know in a day."

This was about building a rapport with Dale, and it started right there with "Hey, do you care if I go to Vegas with you?"

That would mark my first time traveling with the president.

CHAPTER III

Watch Your Language

FROM THE SHEER VOLUME OF phone calls, emails, and text messages I'd received after becoming the crew chief for Dale Earnhardt Jr., I quickly learned there was one truth about his slump: Everyone had an opinion on how to fix it. Most meant well because they loved the guy.

But I'd learned something during my short walk from the conference room table into Rick Hendrick's office, and it was about being in control of your own results. If Rick had said he was firing me because Jeff had gone winless, I wouldn't have been able to argue with that. And even worse, I would have blamed myself because I'd second-guessed myself for not having done things a different way.

My way!

I had been too passive with the way I had run the No. 24 team. I also hadn't followed Jeff's advice about being more assertive.

My philosophy with Dale Jr. would be about generating my own opinion on how to improve his results. If I ever had to make that walk again to Rick's office, I wanted to have done it of my own accord. The worst thing would be to be unsuccessful when I didn't do it my way.

If the Dale Jr. experiment was a complete failure in three years, I would walk out saying, "I don't know what else I could have done." I could look in the mirror at no one else but myself.

As a leader, you can't let anything dictate the circumstances and your fate other than your own opinions. If anything else affects how you go about things, you're just giving yourself excuses that aren't real. It's up to you to make your own opportunities.

With a wife and two kids, I had more of a family life than I ever did at the outset of my tenure as Jeff Gordon's crew chief. Yet I spent a lot more time with Dale than I ever did with Jeff because that was what I thought was necessary to be successful. I explained to Tricia why I was going to do it this way. She supported me, but quite honestly, I didn't care if she understood or agreed.

I just felt she was owed an explanation because I was asking her to accept the sacrifices of my time on our marriage while I worked on my new arranged marriage with Dale Jr.

And Tricia would be accompanying us on the honeymoon, to Las Vegas, appropriately.

* * * * *

It was freezing that early morning at the Statesville airport when we met Dale and his girlfriend (now wife) Amy Reimann. Dale and Amy came blowing in, the pilots grabbed our bags, we all hopped on the plane, and away we went.

I was wearing jeans and a T-shirt, and Tricia was in casual clothes as well, and we were going to the Myers Brothers Awards, which was a suit-and-tie affair. We thought there would be time to change on the way.

But Dale already was in his suit pants.

If I'd known him better, I would have asked him, "Hey, man, why the hell are you wearing your suit pants already? What's the plan for changing into our formalwear?" If it had been four years later, I would have punched him in the arm and said, "Hey, jerk, you're wearing your suit pants already. Thanks for the heads-up on that!"

But this was the honeymoon phase, so I didn't say anything.

When we stopped to get fuel, I politely asked, "When are we putting on our dress clothes?"

"Well, I'm just going to put my jacket on, tie my tie, and I'll be ready to go," Dale says.

Oh.

My poor wife. These are the instances in which she doesn't get enough credit. I thought we would be stopping at a nice hotel to get ready for this event. Instead she got changed in the tiny bathroom of a six-passenger private jet. So did Amy.

This was what life was like with Dale Jr. sometimes.

Dale also had a tendency to use vulgar language. This came up during the flight to Vegas, and Tricia said, "Look, I just want you to know that we have two children, and I have this app that plays your in-car radio broadcasts throughout our whole house. So you really need to work on the language."

And Dale, being the perfect gentleman, responded, "Yes, ma'am. Yes, ma'am." So we laughed about it.

The treatment we received upon arriving in Vegas was no joke. A fleet of black Suburbans pulled up to meet the plane on the tarmac, and a bunch of guys wearing suits waved us inside.

"Don't worry about your luggage, Mr. Earnhardt. We've got it."

We climbed inside an SUV, and they whisked us along the back roads of Las Vegas. We stopped at the service entrance to the Bellagio and then walked through a labyrinth series of hallways, through the kitchen, and then into the ballroom, where the luncheon was being held.

The minute we sat down, the lights came up, and the show began.

It was sort of like a scene straight out of *Goodfellas*. Basically, everything felt like it was waiting on Dale.

Dale gave a terrific speech accepting the award. Someone had spilled coffee on his notes during lunch, so he started out joking that he had some help from Juan Valdez, which no one got, but it was hilarious.

Then he delivered some poignant words while graciously congratulating his teammates Chad and Jimmie on their fifth championship, which he had neglected to remember the previous year.

"I was pretty excited about the award, and every time I win, it's a great honor," Dale said in the speech. "And we were in Vegas for the first time. So that might have had something to do with it. So I want to congratulate Jimmie and Chad. Rick texted me again this morning to make sure I didn't forget! Again. What you guys accomplished is going to resonate through the sport for eternity. It's just amazing what you've been able to do."

When the speech wrapped, Dale went across the hall to talk to the media, and I got my first taste of the magnitude of his popularity. It was about a twenty-foot walk, and yet it was absolute chaos to navigate. Jeff Gordon had a large fan base, too, but that was the first time I'd seen a mob scene around a driver in public like that away from the track.

I was able to eavesdrop on some of Dale's media session. Incredulously, I thought I had overheard him bring up the swearing discussion he'd had with Tricia on the plane.

When we got checked in to the hotel, Tricia got on Google and searched for it, and there it was. Someone asked Dale, "What are you most nervous about?" and he replied, "Well, I'm really nervous that on the way out here, Stevie's wife told me that their kids listen to the team radio, so I'm going to have to clean up my words. I can't cuss anymore."

That was one of the first glimpses I had of a very sincere side of Dale. That had stuck with him, and that was important to me. I joked to Tricia, "Okay, so we've flown for four and a half hours, and that's the no. 1 thing that has resonated with him. He's worried about cussing to my wife and kids?"

I remember thinking, *He's listening!* but *What's he listening to?*

But as the first round of stories began emerging about our relationship from that week, I already could tell we were on the right track in realizing how important it would be to stay connected. Dale was upbeat about wanting changes while speaking graciously and poignantly about his former team, highlighting how everyone would benefit.

"I think it's healthy," he said. "We needed this to happen. I needed this to happen. Hopefully this will get me back to winning races and running in the top five and top ten."

It became clear to me that we really were in the same place professionally. Though I'd come off a mediocre year with Jeff, who had made the Chase and finished ninth in points, going winless was hard on the ego. There was a fear of becoming irrelevant, which was where Dale Jr. had been for two straight seasons.

We were two guys who were scared to death their careers would be over if this didn't work.

Dale also had picked up on some of my tendencies while lightheartedly putting full faith in my leadership style.

He already was trusting me, which allowed me to do my job. He tossed out public compliments, which probably were a little fluffed up because they were in the media, but it was clear that he wanted me to believe them, because Dale doesn't sugarcoat much.

"He's a little bit of a motorboat, talks a lot," Dale said about me with a laugh after the Myers Brothers Award luncheon. "You can't get a word in around him, but if you can hack it, that's about the only bad thing about him. He's got a great disposition and personality. I trust what he's going to be able to do. I tell him every day, whenever we can book time at a track, let's do it. I want to get around the new group and get to know everybody and form the most solid foundation we can relationship-wise throughout the entire team."

That was what I wanted too, but it would require a rigidity to Dale's schedule he had never experienced before in his NASCAR career.

Tricia and I enjoyed our whirlwind trip to Las Vegas with Dale Jr. and Amy (also known as "the first time we traveled with the president") for the 2010 NASCAR Awards Ceremony. **Credit: Letarte Family Collection**

* * * * *

In the first month of 2011, I huddled with Laura Scott and Mike Davis, the two primary keepers of the keys to Dale's schedule, in my office at Hendrick.

These might have seemed minor details, but installing a regimented routine on race weekends was an important part of righting the ship. From researching the situation, I had learned there were days when Dale would show up at the track and go directly to the car. There were others when he would be doing an interview fifteen minutes before getting behind the wheel.

All that would change, because none of it was workable.

"Okay, here's how it is going to work from now on," I told Laura and Mike. "He needs to be in the No. 88 truck and in uniform thirty minutes before practice."

"Why?"

"Because that's when the day starts."

Now the real reason was that I wanted to ensure Dale Jr., not known as the earliest of risers, was awake and hadn't just rolled out of bed. If he walked in groggy, I was going to see it and be on his case to start preparing for practice.

I wanted him to be part of the informal team meeting on race days just before we hit the track. That sometimes could be a logistical nightmare for Dale's handlers because they'd have to navigate an ocean of fans to get him directly to the team hauler from the prerace crew chief–driver meeting. This was important because I didn't want the first time I saw Dale on race day to be at the car just before the green flag.

I also constrained Laura's ability to schedule media, limiting it to certain times during the weekend. Between the end of practice and the start of qualifying, there was a window of at least two hours where Dale wouldn't be doing interviews. He wouldn't be doing anything more than hanging out in the team hauler while we worked to make his car better. Before, Dale had leeway to do as he pleased during that time, but now he'd be an active and constant participant.

It wasn't easy on Laura, whose primary responsibility was making sure the media had time with Dale. He always was sought after for being a great quote in addition to being someone a lot of fans wanted to hear from and read about in stories.

There were stressful situations in which Laura had to beg NASCAR's moderators to stop news conferences that ran long, because she knew she would be answering to me if Dale was late to the hauler.

But she knew that if she caught flak for that, she could send NASCAR's PR reps to me, and I would be happy to tell them that it was in my best interest (and perhaps theirs too) to put Dale in the best position possible to win again. I never had a problem taking that fall, even if it meant facing down the sanctioning body.

The only thing I cared about was getting Dale to concentrate on race cars. If he was having a bad day or needed a nap to refresh, Dale wasn't the sort who would say no to previous obligations.

So I played the bad guy and did it for him.

By installing these rules, it removed any factors that could be left to chance as to whether Dale would be focused on the race weekend's opening practice, which in turn sets the tone for how a team's car qualifies, performs, and races. These were scheduling decisions that might have seemed incidental, but all of them were very strategic.

The goal also was getting Dale to spend more time around the team guys and gain further appreciation for the endless hours they spent on the car. We approached Dale's sister, Kelley, who handled his business affairs, about starting a year-end bonus program for his crew members, as we had with Jeff Gordon.

Since the 1990s, Jeff personally handed out cash bonuses to the crew just for being on the team, but there also were incentives for excellent performances (such as fast pit stops) and winning. Jimmie Johnson also contributed to the pool with Jeff, and it was part of how we did business. The better the team performed, the more the drivers were expected to shell out.

Dale was taking Jeff's place in the shop, and it was essential to continue the same bonus practice if he wanted to become immersed in its winning culture. Dale hadn't paid crew bonuses before, not that he was averse to the idea, but because he didn't understand its necessity.

He immediately was on board once he did—one of many ways in which he and his inner circle embraced our new approach. Unbeknownst to me, Mike already had planted the seeds when he crafted a long email to Dale explaining why he thought aligning with me was his best chance to win a championship.

Mike had been with Dale since 2004 and saw how he had the run of the joint at Dale Earnhardt Inc. Dale could show up late for practice with no repercussions, and those bad habits had lingered even after he'd joined Hendrick.

Under my watch, he would experience a new level of discipline.

But I also wanted to de-emphasize his awareness of being the team's focal point. Because his enormous popularity brought an accompanying amount of attention and time commitments to sponsorships and endorsements, Dale often would get pulled in many directions while also trying to make his car go faster.

The goal was making sure he was the driver for the team and not just the star. At some levels, he wasn't any more important to our success than anyone else who had a role, and I wanted him to appreciate that he just needed to do his job.

Eventually, we grew comfortable enough to compromise on some of the requirements. Sometimes, I'd meet Dale at his motor home instead of at the hauler on race day if it was too difficult to get him there around a sponsor appearance.

But it was important to establish this regimen, and Dale never once cut the corner on what I asked him to do. Not one time.

From talking to those who worked with him in the seasons previous to mine, I knew that things didn't always end well with the crew chief.

But I think Dale felt this was his last chance at being successful in the Cup Series.

Just as it was my second chance at finding redemption for the biggest regret of my career: costing Jeff Gordon his fifth championship.

* * * * *

In 2007, Jeff Gordon and I had one of the greatest seasons in NASCAR history, setting a record that still stands with thirty top ten finishes. But we lost the championship when Jimmie and Chad won four consecutive races in the Chase, breaking our stranglehold on the points and our will in the process.

The next three seasons—my last three with Jeff—were like a fog, because I was haunted by the realization that I had let my best championship shot with a legend slip away, and there wouldn't be another opportunity.

We gave everything we had that year, only to get flat kicked in the teeth. It took a few years for us to understand the emotional toll that took on us. A loss is much worse when you feel as if you've given your best and it's still not good enough.

It's awful for me to say because Jeff was the guy who made me as a crew chief. But he got my worst years atop the pit box. If we could run the 2007 Chase again now, we would have won the title.

If I had those ten races back, I would have prepared the team for the monumental task at hand and not just tried to ignore it. I wouldn't approach that ten-race stretch like any other races, as I originally tried to do.

It would have been presented as a once-in-a-lifetime opportunity, which it really was. After Jeff won two straight races at Talladega and Charlotte, we had a sixty-eight-point lead with only five races remaining. You're standing there with roughly forty days left in the season, with the opportunity to do something that you will remember for the rest of your life, and we didn't treat it like that.

It wasn't my style then to be so assertive, but that shouldn't have stopped me from saying, "This is no longer taking it one race at a time."

On the other side of that race shop, Chad Knaus already had been there. He was selling his guys on, "All you've got to do is give me forty more days. We're this close to making history." It was the speech I should have given.

It was time to get serious and let my guys know that I didn't want to hear about their birthdays or anniversaries or requests for days off. For forty-seven weeks a year, I was their best buddy, and I'd help them through family events, divorces, and marriages. To this day, many of them still call me for advice and help.

But for those five weeks, I should have laid down the law: "I'm not your friend and don't want to hear about anything but racing until the end of the season. Even from Jeff."

We were racing for a championship. I never had been there before as a crew chief, and I didn't handle it right.

Don't get me wrong: Results on Sunday never have been more important than the people I've achieved them with. But I didn't paint the picture of the enormity of what stood before us to those same people on the No. 24. I don't think everyone grasped the enormity of what we were trying to accomplish.

Except for Jeff. He absolutely knew it. And it was a hangover we couldn't shake for the next three years.

Racing for a championship is like being in love. Sometimes, the first person you really fall in love with, you get your heart broken. And that's why people don't fall in love for a few years after that, because it leaves a lingering scar on your heart.

It was the same with losing the 2007 championship. It really sucks when you don't hedge your bets. When you lay everything on the line and it isn't good enough because the other guy wins four consecutive races.

Jeff and I were there. We didn't hold back during that season, and we were honest with each other. Even though I didn't lead the team exactly as I wanted down the stretch, we still gave everything we had at the highest level . . . and walked away with nothing. And then the person that has beat you keeps winning championships, and it makes the hangover worse.

That was where I was when I was aligned with Dale.

He appreciated the opportunity to get a second chance to contend again. But I appreciated it just as much.

And that made us truly appreciate each other more.

CHAPTER IV

Time to Get on Track

THOUGH DALE JR. AND I were in the same place, my years with Jeff had taught me we couldn't be in the same role. It was time to transfer the ownership of the No. 88 team, which previously had belonged to the driver, to the crew chief, in a way I understood.

For all those years I worked on Gordon's team, it was the driver's team. I don't think Jeff ever intended it to be that way. That was just the way it was.

Actually, the best advice Jeff ever gave me about our working relationship was to avoid those dynamics. He wanted *me* to be in charge. He wanted it to be Steve Letarte's team.

But I never took to heart what he said in our first meeting after I was named crew chief of the No. 24 in September 2005. Jeff sat me down and gave me one line of advice.

"Whatever you do, you must treat me like every other person on the team," Jeff told me. "Hold me responsible to my job like every other position."

Did I listen? Nope. I wanted to, but it was hard when the guy talking to you was your mentor. It was my first time as a crew chief, and I didn't handle it right.

Until 2009, all I ever worried about was crew-chiefing. I didn't worry about my personal health, time off, or any well-being. I was very overweight, I never exercised, and the stress of my job and life took over.

29

I accepted that as normal. It wasn't until I retired from being a crew chief in 2014 that I realized that level of stress was abnormal for most people.

I underwent a heart physical, and the doctor told me I was at high risk for health problems if I continued down this destructive path. If I wanted to see my daughter graduate college and get married, I needed to change my approach and lifestyle.

It was a major moment in my career at twenty-eight, the age when many people were just getting started in their professional lives.

In 2009, I lost fifty pounds, began working out with my pit crew, and recommitted myself to my family. I was a different guy. A more mature guy.

It was as much a physical change as an emotional transition. All I did was work before that. When I wasn't at work, I thought about work. I found a way to disconnect from work a little more often, and that allowed me to be more effective and productive.

Working with Dale was also my chance to really listen to Jeff's advice. Unfortunately for Jeff Gordon, it didn't happen with him, but timing isn't always right. Just because you fail to realize the opportunity the first time it's presented doesn't mean you never will have the chance to seize that moment again.

I was now the guy that Mr. H (which is how all Hendrick Motorsports employees refer to the boss) had tasked with rebuilding Dale Jr. This was going to be my team. He was the most popular driver in NASCAR, but he drove for *my* team. I didn't work on Dale Jr.'s team. I would be leading the way.

That was how we approached the first season together, and it was the foundation to my preparation. I decided to leave the team intact as much as possible for the first season with Dale Jr., because how can you prepare for something without being able to evaluate it first?

Preparation is very important, but when you start to talk about people, lives, and careers, those aren't topics in which you make a complete guess, and I didn't have a full understanding of how Dale and I would work together and what we needed. I didn't even have a hunch.

After internally reviewing what we had on the No. 88 team, it was time to take this new approach public, and the preseason media tour would be the platform.

For more than three decades, Charlotte Motor Speedway has been hosting a weeklong media event in January attended by all the nation's top NASCAR reporters to shape their coverage heading into the Daytona 500.

Though it can be monotonous—every driver and team naturally predicts they will excel, win races, and compete for the championship—there also is a method for forming the philosophy of a team, particularly a new one such as mine at the start of the 2011 season.

I had learned over the years that when you talk to the media, it's more than just the fans and sponsors who are reading and watching your words.

You also are talking to your team. They read the coverage more than anyone, and team leaders can't be ignorant to that.

When I tell Jenna Fryer of the Associated Press or Jeff Gluck (formerly of USA Today, now at his own website) something and they write it in an article, it damn well better align with what I'm telling my team in private behind closed doors at Hendrick Motorsports. If those messages aren't aligned, you will face question marks within your team about its real direction.

So I used the 2011 media tour as an opportunity, knowing the right people would be hanging on every word I said. This was my chance to brand the team's identity, and I prepared bullet points to drive it home when Hendrick Motorsports held its media tour stop on January 26, 2011.

When you read through the quotes from that event, the central theme is clear: This was my race team, and Dale was driving for it. There were a lot of great quotes from Dale, Rick Hendrick, and me that asserted the notion that I was in charge of this group.

Every quote was steered toward my taking ownership of the team: "Dale came into *my* shop," "Dale is going to drive *our* cars," "Dale is driving *for me.*"

The goal was to be very clear this wasn't Dale's team. This wasn't Rick's team. This was *my* team. Win, lose, or draw, I was shouldering the responsibility and going out on a limb, or a pedestal, or however you'd want to view it.

It would help insulate Dale from the immense expectations of the outside world and protect him from the enormous pressure that he put on himself.

It really felt as if the world started looking at my team differently.

I put a Google Alert on any story that would have my name and Dale's, and I would spend an hour daily reading through all the articles. I pored over every word he said and measured what the temperament and expectations were around the team.

Reading all of Dale's words also helped me understand his love for speedway racing, and his admiration for Daytona International Speedway and why it was hallowed ground.

It's well-known that it took Dale's father twenty tries to earn his first Daytona 500 victory in 1998, and his death on the last lap of the 2001 Daytona 500 is among the most earth-shattering moments in NASCAR history, prompting a wave of safety advances.

It had been an important place as a driver too for Dale Jr., who won the first race at Daytona after his father's death and triumphed again in the 2004 Daytona 500.

The 2011 Daytona 500 would mark ten years since Dale Earnhardt Sr.'s death, so there were many questions about the race and track during the media tour. Dale Jr.'s quotes about the track's reverence and importance in his life helped me understand him and fill in gaps on what I didn't know.

We later would become great friends who would hang together and drink beer. But at this point, Dale was just a very shy and reserved person around me. I took the initiative to try to accelerate the learning process by any means necessary.

To establish Dale's trust and build his confidence, I knew one way the team could strike immediately was in superspeedway racing. Though it would take a while to improve on the 1.5-mile superspeedways that dominated the Cup circuit, the races at Daytona and Talladega Superspeedway were different.

NASCAR uses a restrictor plate to hold down speeds at both of those tracks through a mandatory reduction of horsepower, and that puts a greater emphasis on the team's input and importance. A well-built car can qualify on pole for the Daytona 500 by virtually anyone with a little practice—you just hold the throttle wide open for one lap.

If we could be fast in qualifying, I knew it would set the tone for the week and put Dale in the right frame of mind. Qualifying at Daytona isn't necessarily about the starting position (a good driver can win from anywhere) or about the publicity; it's about returning the favor to your driver, whom you ask to do crazy things during restrictor-plate races that center around constant risk-taking at maximum speeds.

And when you qualify well, you internally put pressure on the driver to perform with a good car. When a driver qualifies twenty-fifth and doesn't make a daring move to win or gain position, he always can say, "Well, it was because this piece of crap didn't run fast enough."

When Dale Jr. headed down to Daytona, he headed there to win. I knew our team could build him a car that could start on the pole position and have a shot at winning the race, solely through our ingenuity and hard work.

That was where we focused before heading to Daytona International Speedway to begin our first season together. It was very important to Dale, and that made it a priority to me.

* * * * *

Because the No. 88 had finished the 2010 season ranked twentieth in the standings, we were parked on the back side of the garage at Daytona. At that time, NASCAR ordered the team haulers according to their positions in the owner points, and I had been accustomed to having a spot at the front of the garage near all the championship-contending teams.

At Daytona, my team was parked between the numbers 43 and 9 of Richard Petty Motorsports, neither of whom made the 2010 Chase. Nearby were many other midpack or worse teams. It was a culture shock for me. I had never understood the difference between the front and back of the garage, and I fretted over the subsequent impact of the proximity to teams that didn't share our goals or potential.

I made sure the team knew this wasn't our identity. This parking space was temporary, and we'd escape the low-rent district as we began performing this season. My guys weren't going to get comfortable here.

The teams around us would leave early, come in late, and generally have a better time than us, whether it was playing the radio or telling stories or just letting the car sit after practice. Dale's car often would be the only car uncovered early and late in the day during the nearly two weeks that we worked daily in that garage to prepare for the Daytona 500.

I looked like the biggest ass requiring the team to stay later even with nothing essential to do. I made the team clean parts if necessary. We would not leave early. I purposefully was a jerk playing an exaggerated role of drill sergeant because we weren't staying in this part of the garage the rest of the season.

These were the teams Dale had been racing the past two seasons while struggling, and we were changing the mind-set that they were our competition. That new mind-set was the first step in regaining the form we needed to be winners.

* * * * *

Practice started for the Daytona 500, and the first fifteen minutes were the most impressive I'd seen on a restrictor-plate track in my life. Dale went to the back, came to the front, and did virtually anything he wanted with the car.

All those years when he drove Dale Earnhardt Inc. cars that were so good, and I thought they had to be cheating. Now he was driving my car, and I could see how amazing he was.

Dale doesn't talk much about why he is so good at Daytona, and he didn't tell me about it either. He just told me what he needed the car to do. He's just a natural.

It's like Phil Mickelson with the flop shot. People can imitate it, but he still is the best. That's how Dale Jr is with speedway racing. He has a sense for things and anticipates how they will happen beforehand.

So as he zipped through the pack, I watched on top of the truck.

Was he trying to impress us? He made our car seem the fastest there. We build fast cars, but there are a lot of fast teams in the garage. This was about having the best driver, and I instantly couldn't wait for the Daytona 500.

And then the dream basically was extinguished when I saw two cars come roaring by running nose to tail at nearly a second faster than Dale.

It was the beginning of two-car tandem drafting, and we were screwed.

Our cars weren't built for that style of racing. We had the wrong radiators and water systems. Dale also didn't like needing a partner to race well (nor did I). We instantly went from being the favorite to having no chance at winning unless we could get things turned around.

The two-car tandems weren't embraced by fans, and NASCAR would get rid of them a year later. It was so completely abstract compared with anything we'd ever done.

You needed a partner to run well. It would be like waking up one day and realizing you needed to drive on the wrong side of the road to get to work. It was so ridiculous. No one liked to do it, even the people doing it well, but you had to do whatever it took to win.

The tandems wouldn't matter in single-car qualifying for the Daytona 500, though. Our car captured the pole, and Jeff Gordon took the other front-row spot.

A great way to get things started: Qualifying on pole for the 2011
Daytona 500 alongside our teammate. It was Dale's third start
from the front row in the Great American Race.
Credit: Harold Hinson Photography

We flew home that Sunday night with the pole trophy in tow.
Driving out of the track, we took a picture of the pylon with our
number at the top. We took in that moment. It was a big deal for our
team and all of Hendrick Motorsports.

That Monday, I walked around the entire team complex with
the trophy, taking photos with it and employees in the chassis shop,
the body shop, the engine shop. Dale was a popular driver, but he had
only one win in his first three seasons with Hendrick Motorsports.

Not only did I have to win over the driver, but damn, I also
had to win over the entire company. It was one more step toward our
ultimate goal. The employees at Hendrick would do anything you
asked of them because that's how they are, but I wanted them to do
it before I asked. You do that by showing some appreciation of their
hard work.

Just like having a deliberate strategy on the media tour, there
were very specific reasons I made that victory tour around the shop.
We were celebrating the pole, but we also were going to have Dale Jr.
be everybody's favorite on every level for all the right reasons. There

was an unspoken culture of doubt in Dale's ability at Hendrick that I wanted to change.

The beauty of having a win-at-all-costs company such as Hendrick is no one cares about the baloney. They don't want to hear about how nice of a guy a driver is or how much sponsorship money they bring to the company. They don't give a crap about that kind of stuff.

All they care about is *results*.

It's ice-cold for people who never have seen it. There are people who don't cut it at Hendrick because nobody talks around the water cooler about how good you are unless you win. It's intimidating. You're measured at a different level at that company. It's won a record twelve Cup championships.

This wasn't a team built on good results; it was built on winning and championships, which was why I loved being raised there.

Hendrick Motorsports now had to apply that win-at-all-costs philosophy to changing our Daytona 500 cars on the fly for tandem drafting in the limited practice sessions before the race. Unfortunately, it didn't go well.

We had to ask Dale to put the car in awful positions to test out the new cooling systems and different radiators. Two days after winning the pole, we crashed in the first practice back on Wednesday. Dale never would have been in those positions if I hadn't asked him to test the car's limits.

If I had asked Jeff to do that a year earlier, he would have said, "No way, I'm going to crash!" But Dale would have done anything I asked him to do. At that time, I didn't realize it. Because what I'd asked him to do—push the water temperatures to the max to test the radiators—was asinine.

Dale came into the garage, I put my arm around him, and I said, "All right, let's unload the other one."

As the team prepared the backup car, I could see the culture of the team was already changing and what I'd tried to establish was taking root. One of our IT guys, Brad, whose nickname was Two Gig, was helping take out the engine. So was Doug Duchardt, one of our top executives. And Dale Jr. was helping too.

I thought to myself, *You know what? They all get it.* The IT guy, who didn't know the difference between any wrench in the tool-box, was helping take the engine out under Dale's direction. This group finally got it, and Dale saw they would believe in him when the results and speed were there.

Dale looks over a pole-winning car that never started the race.
Credit: Harold Hinson Photography

That was the moment in which I realized I could shift my focus from changing the culture back to solely focusing on improving the car's performance. Everyone knew and understood the goal.

I think my hard work, my perseverance, and being a little bit of a jerk in setting the tone during Speedweeks had paid off. When things went as bad as possible, we still stood together as a team with the same goal.

* * * * *

Dale and I had a serious discussion in his motor home about whether we should even race in the Thursday qualifier that set the

LEADING THE WAY

field for the Daytona 500. Because of a bizarre NASCAR rule, as a Daytona 500 pole-sitter that crashed before the qualifier, we would start from the rear of the Daytona 500 no matter our result in the qualifying race.

He was really quiet, still not fully comfortable with asserting his opinion, and kept saying, "Whatever you want to do." Finally, I was like, "All right, we're going to race the hell out of it."

Looking back, it was a great choice because it instantly showed Dale we believed in him, especially when times got tough. We believed he could do it. I told him, "Here's the deal. We know we're starting last and don't need to win, but we're going to need to learn a lot for Sunday. Go race. If we crash again, that's fine. If you get to a spot you don't like and lift the accelerator, that's fine. I'm going to support whatever you do."

Dale finished thirteenth.

Our first Daytona 500 together was just okay. Dale got a flat tire late in the race, pitted out of sequence, and crashed, finishing twenty-fourth. It was the only Daytona 500 we didn't finish first or second in our four seasons together.

Daytona was over. Now it was time for reality. We were leaving the comfort of the speedways, where Dale had found success four times annually, and heading to the downforce racetracks, where he had struggled. Those were the venues that made up most of the season, and it would be where our team and trust were tested.

* * * * *

We unloaded our car in the next race at Phoenix and were so slow. We qualified thirty-fifth and never found anything to make it better. But we kept our heads down and kept fighting to finish tenth.

It was an improvement, but I realized there was reason for concern. You can't be that slow and hope that things will keep falling your way as they did for us during the course of that race.

The race the next weekend was at Las Vegas Motor Speedway, the first of the 1.5-mile tracks that comprise the majority of the season. You can't win the championship unless you excel at these tracks,

39

where aerodynamics and horsepower are critical.

Dale had a love-hate relationship with the 1.5-mile tracks, and it hadn't been good lately. In 2004, two weeks after winning the Daytona 500, Dale endured one of the worst races of his life at Las Vegas, completing only 196 of 267 laps and finishing thirty-fifth after parking the car because its handling was so bad.

That same season, he entered the finale at Homestead-Miami Speedway with a shot at the title but with virtually no confidence at the track. He finished twenty-third.

This would be a critical weekend for our team at Las Vegas, and it didn't start with sparkles and sunshine. The car came off the hauler with average speed, and we stayed that way in qualifying.

Something happened the next day after Saturday practice, though. We debriefed in the lounge of our hauler, and then Dale stayed while I watched the Xfinity Series race with engineer Kevin Meendering.

This was unscripted.

Normally, Dale would head back to his motorhome instead of hanging with us, but this time he stayed there and watched the race while weighing in on the discussion that I was having with Kevin about the car's setup. We would talk, and then Kevin would spin around in his chair and ask Dale questions about the handling.

Hendrick Motorsports does personality studies of all its employees, and it organizes them by colors. Dale and Rick Hendrick are both blues, which means they need time to digest questions. With Rick, you can ask for something, and it may take a week to get a call after he fully considers it. Dale Jr.'s personality has the exact same trait. He needs time to soak in the information.

So while we were sitting there, he still was processing the information from practice, saying, "I might have said this earlier, but maybe the car was doing that instead." We learned then how important it was just to give him some time and space about what we were doing. And it worked this time, thank goodness.

If we'd run poorly, maybe he never would have believed in me again.

That night before the race in Vegas, I went to dinner with Dale and Amy at a Japanese steak house on the Las Vegas Strip. I remember getting so frustrated with Saturday night traffic and going crazy at red lights, while Dale just sat there as patient as he could be.

"How can this not bother you?" I asked.

"Man, what are you going to do?" He smiled, playfully picking on me.

It was a good example of bonding for no other reason than we should. It allowed us to work at our relationship away from the stress of the racetrack, and that was important for everyone.

It's very hard to have a great and healthy relationship in a competitive environment. I purposely pulled him away from the uncomfortable, pressure-filled garage area to develop our relationship and trust away from those decisions and situations. That helped it become real.

The next day in the race, after making adjustments based on Dale's feedback, we had a top-three car. When everyone took two tires at the end, I went conservative with four, and we finished eighth because of it. We probably could have been in the top five, but it was about taking baby steps.

We had talked all winter about commitment and what it takes to be better, and many of those things had happened during the first month on the track, from everyone pitching in at Daytona to Dale hanging in our hauler to talk setup for hours at Vegas.

Years later, Dale explained to his fans why he chose to stay in the hauler. It was because of concern about our speed in practice and the results at Daytona and Phoenix.

"I'm getting real nervous," Dale said, recalling that day. "Like, 'Okay, this isn't working. What's going to happen to me?' I'd been going to the hauler early. So after the last practice, I said, 'I'm not leaving this hauler until they leave it.' And we sat in there for six hours. That was the moment that 'Man, this is going to work great.' All I need to do is do exactly what Steve told me, and that's be there and be accountable and be available."

I didn't ask Dale to stay that Saturday in Vegas, but he did, and we finished better because of it.

It was more proof that actions don't just speak louder than words. *They deliver.*

CHAPTER V

Six Damn Ounces

THE NEXT TWO RACES WERE relatively uneventful. Dale finished eleventh at Bristol Motor Speedway and twelfth at Auto Club Speedway, and they were good weeks for maintaining our team cohesion and consistency, but it was nothing special.

Until Martinsville Speedway.

At 0.526 miles, it's the shortest track on the circuit, but it means more to me than any other as a place with so many special memories. I earned my first win as a crew chief in October 2005 there with Jeff Gordon. It also had been a track of great triumph and tragedy for Hendrick Motorsports (a team plane crashed on the way to a race there in 2004, killing ten).

When we unloaded on this April 2011 weekend with Dale, everything was business as usual, though business as usual at the track was very different for me compared with what it had been for Dale in many years.

We were good, not great, but we stuck with it and grinded through the weekend. We didn't have a winning car Sunday, but much like in Phoenix, we stuck with the plan we'd discussed, which was just continue to keep our heads down and work hard.

I'd reviewed the notes of Dale's recent races at Martinsville, and there was a pattern in which he started laying excuses during his radio conversations long before the race even started ("Well, I told you about this in practice" was a familiar refrain when things went wrong).

Dale had been so confident it would go wrong he started building in excuses from the word *go*.

I told him we weren't going to have excuses. I didn't want to hear during Sunday's race about something that had been wrong on Saturday. If we were running poorly, I just wanted him to tell me what needed to be fixed. And not tell me how it was off the day before too.

Much like most things in life and business, races are long, drawn-out affairs, and it is very hard to continue to see the light through the end of the process. It's so muddy and murky, and it takes forever.

A five-hundred-lap race at Martinsville is a lot like that. I think that's why I love this track. You have to break down these races into very small parts that the brain can comprehend and that you can digest, because if you try to look at the entirety of five hundred laps, it'll overwhelm you.

For the longest time, I thought this applied only to me and my ADD-type personality requiring smaller goals to function at a higher level. But what I've learned is it's really not just me. This applies to most of the human race. We cannot focus on the now without being distracted by what's next. It's how the whole world is, right?

So my job was to worry about what was next as the leader of the team. I had to have the vision. All I wanted the team to work on was the here and right now. I wanted my tire changer to work on the current pit stop. I wanted my driver to work on the current lap.

Let me be the visionary. Don't cloud any of your actions with the concern of the future, because that is my job. I need everybody to do their job and not someone else's.

And that was really what the team did. They focused on the now and worked on the small goals, one after another, until reaching the ultimate objective. That was exactly what we needed that day at Martinsville, because it gave us the chance to win.

This was another major step, and it made the whole system that we'd implemented seem especially real to Dale, because he loves Martinsville and knows how challenging it is. If I had said on Friday (when we qualified twenty-sixth), "We're going to have a chance to win this race," his answer would have been, "You're crazy."

It would have been the same answer after practice Saturday. And on lap 100. Probably even lap 300.

But with twenty laps remaining, Dale took the lead from Kyle Busch and did it while looking like his old man. I remember thinking, *This is awesome, we're going to run like second or third,* and Dale was thinking of more.

He hardly tried to pass Kyle. It was basically "I think you're better than me, but listen, buddy: You've won a lot, and I haven't, and I'm going to move you." So up the track Kyle went and into the lead went Dale Jr.

After that, it's simple, right? Lead the last twenty laps and pull into victory lane.

But it's like shooting free throws in an empty gym versus shooting free throws to win a game. If you've never had to perform with a game on the line, that's a hell of a shot to make.

You don't win by getting in the right spot just once; you win by getting in the right spot time and time and time again until you know how to handle each situation. It had been nearly three years since Dale's last victory, and he basically just tried too hard when Kevin Harvick began applying pressure in the closing laps.

We weren't good enough to be in front of Kyle, and Dale had beat the crap out of his car to take the lead. So with three laps remaining, Dale overdrove the car in the third turn like a qualifying lap, completely missing the bottom, and Harvick went by us for the lead, entering the first turn of the next lap.

Dale hung on for second—his best finish in more than a year.

When he walked out of Martinsville, he could not deny we were four laps from winning. No bullshit. It was stamped as fact. We came in with a plan, we focused on it, and the plan paid dividends.

Two months earlier before the season, I said our goal was to be relevant. We wanted to be on TV because the team was good, not because it had Dale Earnhardt Jr. behind the wheel.

Six races into 2011, we were there. We actually were more than relevant. We had a chance to win. Our whole system was real, and Dale knew it.

* * * * *

The lessons learned at Martinsville quickly benefited the entire company. Two weeks later, we were back to tandem racing at Talladega. We hadn't been prepared at Daytona, but damn, were we ready this time. It wouldn't take us by surprise again.

Chad and I made a plan that Jimmie and Dale had to work together to get one of the cars into victory lane. We would pit together, would restart together, and stayed lined up together for five hundred miles. We never discussed the finish and who should be leading—we just let it play out. And sure enough, Dale was in the support role and did exactly what the company needed him to do, even if it wasn't necessarily what the team needed.

The No. 88 couldn't win in the position we were in, so Dale pushed Jimmie to the win. It was purely circumstantial that his car was the trailer on the final lap. It didn't matter to Dale that it was— he saw the larger picture of what a checkered flag meant for Hendrick Motorsports, which had only one win in the first eight races.

And looking back, this was a race that built the foundation that would pay returns for so long. It was Dale buying into "I'm part of the team, and I'm going to do what's necessary."

He filled the role the company needed.

* * * * *

The Coca-Cola 600 is one of the crown jewels in NASCAR: The Daytona 500, the Southern 500, the Brickyard 400, and the Coke 600. All races are important, but those four stand above the rest because of their history and the significance of the racetracks.

Memorial Day weekend is a racer's dream. It begins early in the morning with the Grand Prix of Monaco, a Formula One showcase on the streets of Monte Carlo. Then the afternoon brings the greatest spectacle in racing, the Indianapolis 500. It concludes with NASCAR's longest race of the season at the track in the hub of stock-car activity—a couple of miles from Hendrick Motorsports headquarters.

On that afternoon, the No. 88 team gathered in the lounge of the hauler and watched the Indy 500 while preparing for our race in the evening. J. R. Hildebrand's car, which was sponsored by the

National Guard, just like ours, hit the fence while leading off the final turn.

I'm friends with John Barnes, the owner of that car, so I texted him, "Man, I'm really sorry," and I remember him saying something like, "Well, man, you're going to have to go get a win." It was a nice little pep talk and led us into our strategizing for a race that is a four-hour marathon beginning in daylight and ending under the lights.

We talked about how our system had worked in another long race at Martinsville and that we would approach it the same way: just by keeping our heads down.

Just like Martinsville, there were hardly any early highlights. We were just okay for the first five hundred miles. That's the grind of the six hundred. You keep reiterating, "I know it's six hundred miles," because you know no matter how many times you tell yourself that, you haven't said it enough. That race is infinitely longer than you can dream. At times, it's miserably long.

In the closing laps, fuel strategy came into play. I was sitting on the top of the pit box and proud of our effort. We had stuck to our system, stayed on the lead lap, and done everything we needed to do, and I really wanted to reward the team.

Our fuel mileage numbers said we needed a certain number of laps under yellow flags to stretch it to the finish. Cars get better mileage under caution—the general rule of thumb is you consume as much fuel in two laps under yellow versus one lap under green.

So I said, "To hell with it! We're going to take the gamble." There are times you have to lead and make decisions as a crew chief that really will end up defining your career, your legacy, and how others think of you. No matter how well prepared you are and how many people are there to help, there's no manual for being a true leader.

This was a gamble that would define us. If we came up short, we could suffer a poor finish that would wreck all the momentum built by our methodical approach that season. But if we were to win, it would be a validating breakthrough.

I made the decision that we wouldn't pit. At this point, it doesn't matter if you're in sports, business, or any line of work. You can prepare all you want, but at some point, you have to suck it up and say,

46

"This is the plan." I can remember it as clear as day as Kasey Kahne's car ran out of fuel. We took the lead on a green-white-checkered restart, meaning there were two laps to go.

That was three miles from victory lane.

But I also knew we hadn't gotten enough laps under yellow to feel secure. As the enthusiasm of the team and the crowd built around me at the white flag because of the big lead from a great restart by Dale Jr., I was thinking, *We're screwed.*

But two turns later, he still led by fifteen car lengths. I ruled out all doubt. We were going to win.

Oh, if only that flag were black AND white (as in checkered). But Dale wouldn't be in the lead after the next and final trip around Charlotte Motor Speedway in the 2011 Coca-Cola 600. **Credit: Harold Hinson Photography**

For about five seconds, I was as excited as my crew. I looked down, and they were standing on top of the pit wall, looking toward turn 4, praying they would see their car return first.

There's no fuel gauge in a Cup car, so we had no way of knowing how close we were. There are assumptions built upon assumptions, that the team knows exactly how much fuel was put in the car on each of the ten pit stops.

While math is an exact science, fuel mileage is not.

Dale ran out of fuel at the end of the backstretch on the final lap, losing the lead to Kevin Harvick and finishing seventh. The difference between that and winning was six ounces of fuel, or about half of a soda can. A grande cup of Starbucks filled with an E15 blend would have gotten us to victory lane.

There were a lot of assumptions made trying to find whether we had those six freaking ounces, and it was agonizing for the team.

Consider for a minute what these guys had been through. They had a future Hall of Fame driver in Jeff Gordon. Then they lost Jeff Gordon. Now they had Dale Jr., and he was so close to winning for the first time in 104 races.

It was a kick in the gut, to say the least. I'd asked them to work night and day and commit so much to building this system, and we were this close.

And then we ran out of fuel.

My heart was broken. The team had performed. The driver had performed. I felt like I let them down.

It was my call to gamble on mileage, and it didn't work.

Fortunately, seventh still wasn't too bad. And most importantly, I learned an even greater lesson in the way Dale handled it. We'd seen his temper tantrums and rants on the team radio in past seasons. But when he climbed out and did interviews, he said the car was great, showed confidence in his team, and supported me for taking the risk.

That was the moment.

Everyone thinks, *Oh, it was about almost winning,* but it really wasn't. It actually was how Dale handled not winning that continued the course of action for the team. Because that support he gave me after the race was really the push I needed to be the leader.

I'd orchestrated this grand plan since the media tour as the leader of the team, but I still felt a little like a puppet. While I was the crew chief and calling the shots, was I running the team my own way?

I promised myself after my years with Jeff Gordon that I was only going to do this my way. The gamble on fuel at Charlotte was the first time I said this was purely on me. It was the type of decision that I wouldn't have made with Jeff. There was no life preserver.

The moment Dale supported me in defeat was one of the major reasons we continued on. It was just like once the ball was in motion, I didn't have to reassure him about things. We could just focus on going fast.

From the time the team worked on the crashed car in practice at Daytona to when Dale stayed in the lounge at Las Vegas to when we grinded it out in Martinsville.

Each time was a test of "Hey, we know you can race, and we believe in you." Then at Charlotte, it didn't work out, yet he stayed on board and believed in *me*. That was really the bonus of that night in what was a crushing defeat.

That night was one of the biggest reasons that we won races together.

CHAPTER VI

A Tap on the Shoulder

THOUGH IT WAS A DISAPPOINTMENT, the Coca-Cola 600 marked nearly the midpoint of the regular season, and Dale was in great shape for making the playoffs for the first time in three years.

Through twelve of twenty-six races in the regular season, we were fourth in points. A runner-up finish the next week at Kansas Speedway—Brad Keselowski barely beat us by stretching his last tank of fuel with better mileage—improved us to third in points heading into the summer.

But the stretch from June through August felt extremely long, and we struggled. We had made a plan that we executed to perfection in the first half of the regular season, but the plan we had for the summer never worked.

Over the last dozen races—from the June 19 race at Michigan through the September 10 race at Richmond—Dale finished in the top ten only once (a ninth at Pocono in August).

As the summer wore on, I wondered if I was doing the right things. It tested my patience. It tested my will. It felt as if we were working *so* hard, as hard as the first three months of the season, but we weren't gaining any ground.

Naturally, the doubt crept in, and I began to worry. "Was our great start just a fluke?" Man, every race was like one kick in the gut after another. I looked back at our early highlights and questioned whether they were rewards for working hard, or if they had been strokes of good fortune, that skewed our opinions of our progress and ability.

What if we actually were going down the same path that led Dale to mediocre seasons in 2009 and 2010?

Those were the thoughts I wrestled with as we entered the regular-season finale at Richmond International Raceway, which determined the twelve drivers who would make the Chase. This was a defining moment in the season. Qualifying for NASCAR's playoffs—the only way to race for the championship—has become viewed as the ultimate validation of whether your team had a good season.

Though Dale had rebounded early in the season with some strong results at Kansas, Charlotte, and Martinsville, it largely would be forgotten if we didn't seal the deal and claim a playoff berth to confirm his status as a title contender. If the team missed the Chase, Dale still would run the final ten races for pride, but it would be followed by persistent questions about our summer-long fade.

The good news was, Dale didn't have to do much to lock in a Chase berth. Regardless of how anyone behind him fared, as long as he finished twentieth or better, he would be in the Chase. In twenty-four previous starts at Richmond, Dale had finished worse than twentieth only four times and he had won three times. It was among his favorite tracks on the circuit.

We were okay in practice but qualified poorly in twenty-seventh. It's the last place you want to start on a tight short track. You will be in trouble if there is a wreck early. And there was.

On the eighth lap, there was a thirteen-car crash in the fourth turn. It was like watching in slow motion from my vantage point atop the pit box. Clint Bowyer let his foot off the brake of his No. 33 Chevrolet. The car rolled slowly down the banking, and Dale ran square into him.

And then the battle really was on. We had to make multiple pit stops to repair the nose, and we kept pitting at every opportunity to improve the car, manage the fight, and give us a chance.

The longest night of my NASCAR life on one of the shortest tracks in the series: Here's the beginning of the wreck that led to numerous repairs and one memorable pep talk. **Credit: Harold Hinson Photography**

Not long after the crash, Dale was a lap down and fighting to be in position to get back on the lead lap if a caution came out. He ran into the back of David Gilliland, trying to gain a spot, making the damage even worse, and causing a yellow. NASCAR wouldn't give Dale his lap back because the caution was his fault.

I was shocked. I thought, *What the hell? Did he not understand the goal? Did he not understand what we're doing here? He is going to punch a hole in the radiator and throw away everything we've worked for in one night."*

I was losing the one thing I usually am best with: patience. I had lost it.

As things were unraveling on the track, I was unraveling on the pit box. I couldn't keep the calm that I needed.

The summer had gone on too long. We had fought so hard, and nothing was going right. It felt as if it all was coming to a head on the evening we were supposed to be celebrating making the playoffs and affirming a remarkable turnaround.

We were throwing it all away.

Then I got some much-needed advice and encouragement from an unexpected source.

It wasn't from Rick Hendrick, one of the greatest leaders I had known. It wasn't from Ken Howes, Hendrick Motorsports's vice president of competition and my mentor and longtime adviser.

It was from Marshall Carlson, the team's president, who is known for being an affable sort with a sometimes-goofy sense of humor.

He climbed atop our pit box about two-thirds of the way through the race. Picture a football sideline where the offensive coordinator, defensive coordinator, and head coach frantically are trying to stop the bleeding as their team lets a win slip away. I was playing all those roles at once, and I wasn't doing a good job.

I was beyond frustrated and really wasn't giving my best. I was at a mental breaking point when Marshall tapped me on the shoulder. I spun around and shot him an angry look that said, "What are you doing up here?"

And he very calmly reminded me what I had accomplished in building that team. He explained we could look at this situation in dismal terms, or another way was to look at how *close* we were to achieving something great.

Think about it differently. Say, you had been off all year long but went to Richmond with a chance and then had your best run ever there.

The math still was the same.

He basically just reminded me that we were on the cusp of accomplishing an incredible goal that we would have laughed at nine months earlier.

It was like a dose of refreshingly cold water splashed in my face. I instantly was calm, appreciative, and refocused. Dale somehow battled his way to sixteenth, and more importantly, we qualified for our first Chase together.

A patch job that was good enough to finish 16th and make the Chase. Results depended on all… from the soothing words of Marshall Carlson to the guys fixing the damage. **Credit: Harold Hinson Photography**

This was the *only* time in my ten seasons as a Hendrick crew chief that Marshall Carlson ever tapped me on the shoulder to offer advice during a race. The conversation might have lasted thirty seconds, but sometimes great advice can come in the form of powerful words spoken to an eager group. Or sometimes it can just be a simple reminder between two people at exactly the right time.

When you hear me on TV breaking down a race or making a point while speaking at a conference, you'll hear me use "Results depend on all."

This example is exactly what I mean. Marshall does a great job in his role, but he mostly stays involved with the business side of racing instead of the competition. He worked for many years at Hendrick Automotive Group before returning to racing to handle business affairs after the 2004 plane crash in which the team lost president John Hendrick and general manager Jeff Turner.

Marshall admittedly doesn't have the racing experience of many in the organization. He might have seemed precisely the opposite person you'd expect to provide that kind of advice, but his was timed correctly and exactly.

With everyone in any walk of life—whether it's a race team or a business—it can be time to receive advice or time to give the advice. Sometimes the right advice at the right time is much more important than who delivers it.

You don't have to be the CEO or star player on the team to deliver those words of wisdom.

* * * * *

I would love to say we carried momentum into the Chase and went on to win the championship, but we didn't. Dale took third in the rain-postponed opener at Chicagoland Speedway and didn't finish in the top five again over the final nine races.

To be honest, we really didn't even have a chance at the title, and we finished seventh in points. It wasn't a storybook ending. But that wasn't the point.

The point was, we made the playoffs, and that was a great accomplishment.

When we left the finale at Homestead-Miami Speedway, I was on empty and gassed out mentally and physically. I never had missed a Hendrick Motorsports Christmas party, but Tricia and I decided to take the family all the way to Hawaii that December because we needed a major recharge.

I don't think Tricia had any idea how much she helped me. I was gone all the damn time while trying to establish a personal relationship with Dale that benefited our professional relationship. Even when I was at home, I was calling, emailing, and texting him. Dale would call up and say, "Hey, man, what are you doing? Come up and have a beer." It'd be midnight, and I'd get in my car and go up there to hang out with him.

It was abnormal in that it wasn't a typical work relationship. This was a lifestyle shift, and he made huge sacrifices to get out of his comfort zone. I made sacrifices too.

But my family made the biggest sacrifices. We had a three-on-three basketball league that I played in with Dale that couldn't have been at a worse time for my family with two kids—Tuesday nights at 7. But I'd play every year, and afterward, we'd drink beer and hang out.

As witnessed in the example with Marshall Carlson, results can depend on everyone at every level, not only with Marshall's poignant advice, but also with my wife and children allowing me to pursue this path. They didn't force me to make decisions.

So we skipped the Christmas party that year so I could take Tricia and my kids to Hawaii and reward them for how much they indirectly had played an important role in the team's success. I don't know if Tricia and my family have any idea how much they helped rebuilding the No. 88 team. What they gave up was huge, and sometimes the support staff for a group plays as an important role as the group's employees.

In Hawaii, we completely unplugged.

* * * * *

Well, sort of. As the leader of a team or the boss of a company, you realize that you're somehow always on duty. The team needed a new tire specialist, and Rob Lopes, the leading candidate, happened to be in Maui on vacation with his wife as well.

So I called him, and he decided to come visit my resort. I interviewed him at our condo, and let me tell you, the sales pitch doesn't have to be that strong with a cold Corona in your hand and a view of the Pacific Ocean. He joined the team for the next season.

And when we returned, I learned at a kickoff luncheon for the 2012 season that I had received the Papa Joe Hendrick Award of Excellence for the first time.

It's funny that this was the first time we missed the Christmas party, because the Papa Joe Hendrick Award is one of the big moments of that event, and in all the years I'd gone, I never had been nominated for the award (which started in 1995).

Anyone can be put up for consideration by any Hendrick employee. There are boxes with forms set up around the Hendrick Motorsports campus. Out of five hundred employees, usually there are twenty to thirty who are nominated, and before they announce the winner, they announce all the nominees and recognize them. But I hadn't been recognized yet.

This is the most prestigious award at Hendrick, because it's who best embodies and endears the spirit of Papa Joe, the patriarch of the entire team as Rick's late father. It's given to the team member who displays outstanding job performance, leadership, teamwork and contributions above and beyond expectations to help the organization succeed.

There are some very important and noteworthy winners: vice president of competition, Ken Howes; team manager Brian Whitesell; longtime engineer Jim Wall; crew chief Chad Knaus. Even Rick Hendrick himself.

In 2011, I was the winner, along with Jeff Gordon. And that meant a lot to win it in the same year with him, because it was the first season we hadn't worked together since 2005, and we both had made sacrifices for the company.

But Jeff received his honor at the Christmas party. I didn't get mine until a luncheon a few months later at the beginning of the 2012 season.

When you're a crew chief, you generally don't have time during the season for these luncheons because they usually are just intended to get everybody together to sing "Kumbaya" about how great a year it was. I was trying to get my hauler loaded for the next race.

But I naturally went after being asked. And Tricia was there, and my parents were there. The recognition really sank in when I saw them.

In the racing world, the accolades can come sparingly. You're either fast or slow. You either win or lose. And much of the time, what you did wrong is highlighted by the news media.

So a peer-nominated award like this means the world. It's recognition that you aren't just beating your head against the wall. People see the good you're doing.

Ken Howes, who is a man of few words, spoke on my behalf. He is a mentor to me, and it really meant a lot. They have a committee that chooses the award, and when my name finally came up for nomination, Ken said, "Well, we can't give it to Stevie again, he already has won it."

Ken's point was that I was a fixture and that I was always in a good mood. So people always figured, "Well, someone else will nominate Stevie, everyone knows him. I'll nominate someone in the teardown shop or wherever instead."

I was caught off guard. I was too emotional to deliver a good acceptance speech. I wasn't in the right mind-set, which made it even more special. I was focused on preparing for the next race, and this was just one more example that sometimes it's good to stop and enjoy the moment.

As I walked to the podium to receive the award, Jeff Gordon stood up and began to clap, leading the standing ovation. The fact that it was him leading it meant even more.

Jeff and I have a different relationship than I had with Dale. Though Jeff is a friend, we don't hang out the way I've had with Dale. Jeff and I worked great together in racing, but we had less of a bond socially.

We were sort of one of those couples that seemed great on paper but doesn't have the same personal chemistry.

So it meant a lot to have Jeff be so supportive—just the way he had been when I became the crew chief of his car, because he approved it. I wouldn't be where I am today or receive that award without his help.

Basically, Hendrick had been my entire world outside of my family since I was sixteen. Anyone I respected, considered a mentor or a father figure, or wanted to make proud, they all voted to give me that award. It's like coaches anointing a star athlete in high school as the best.

All this happened barely a year after I thought Rick Hendrick was firing me. You just have to trust that you're on the right path and keep grinding away. You also have to hold true to your moral compass. Even though this award isn't a championship, this was the first trophy that Dale and I earned together.

That Papa Joe Hendrick Award is now in my office, next to my Daytona 500 trophy. It means a ton to me. I had worked at Hendrick Motorsports for sixteen years then, and now I was being honored with this great award.

It was a great way to finish that first season with Dale.

One of the most important trophies I've received… named after the late father of the man presenting it to me. To embody the spirit of Papa Joe Hendrick is a high accolade. **Credit: Letarte Family Collection**

CHAPTER VII

Pushing the Button

MY FIRST SEASON WITH DALE was an unqualified success, but it would have been hard not to have exceeded the expectations, because they were virtually nonexistent entering 2011. Yes, Dale had run much better and gained fourteen positions in the points standings (seventh, his best ranking in five years), but we still had a long way to go.

If we didn't back it up and improve, 2011 would have been regarded as a gimmick that just happened to work: "Yeah, they're throwing one more thing at Dale Jr., we'll see if it sticks."

This sounded familiar.

When I became Jeff Gordon's crew chief with ten races remaining in the 2005 season, the late *Charlotte Observer* reporter and columnist David Poole wrote that I was the next Pete Rondeau, who was Dale Jr.'s crew chief for only eleven races.

A few days before my first race with Gordon at New Hampshire, Poole, who was among the most respected media members in NASCAR, wrote that I wouldn't even last as long as Rondeau. I was just Hendrick's bridge to the next real plan.

I didn't know Poole that well (though I'd come to like and admire him like many others for his willingness to be opinionated and outspoken), and I tacked his story to the board behind my desk at the No. 24 shop, where it stayed every day that I was a crew chief at Hendrick (I still have the article to this day).

I didn't tell the world at that time, but that was my inspiration. Here was someone entrenched in the sport who didn't think I could do this. I had to prove him and everyone else wrong.

It was a similar challenge to what I and Dale were facing in our second season together.

We moved the needle enough in 2011 that expectations sky-rocketed in 2012. We were no longer off the radar. We would have to prove worthy of the attention.

It was time to tweak the team to suit Dale's needs. We didn't make many of those changes in the first year for fear of being too disruptive. Now we had a solid baseline that would allow us to work on making the driver comfortable.

The foundation was there because team owner Rick Hendrick had made the call to pair Dale and me. In his typically classy manner, Mr. Hendrick deflected all the credit. He never would point at that and beat his chest to say, "Look at what I did!" Instead, it was, "Stevie is the perfect fit."

Mr. Hendrick has an incredible talent for speaking from the heart like a simple guy from Virginia, but while he has such a down-home, country-boy charisma, he also has the precision of a surgeon when it comes to choosing the perfect words—but not seeming overt about the methods. He is the world's greatest puppeteer without seeming as if he ever has a string in his hands.

His comments about my work meant the world to me, but I wanted the world to know how much everyone within the team had sacrificed to improve. A plan is only as good as how it's being executed, and we were fortunate to have a group of people who dedicated themselves to perfect execution. That's why I remain so close to many of those on that 2011 team, because they sacrificed so much for the greater good of becoming a winner.

The team's selflessness also was appreciated by Dale, whose comments in the 2012 preseason were very telling. He affectionately spoke about how he liked the discipline I'd instilled in the team and said he hadn't realized how much he had missed it to that point in his career until experiencing that regimentation.

I had wondered what he thought of all the structure. He had been an active participant, but did he really believe in it? I never asked him if he liked it. I don't set my son's bedtime at nine and then ask what he thinks about that.

Would Dale Jr. credit the changes? My answer came quickly while reading his preseason comments:

> Steve said, "Look, there's a lot of things I'm going to expect you to do, and I need you here at this time. I need you at the truck this early." There was a lot of stuff, and I'd never been under those kinds of guidelines before. I'd always kind of gotten my way and done it how I wanted to do it. I knew last year that if it doesn't work with Steve, the excuse basket is kind of getting empty. So I need to apply myself and do what this guy tells me to do. I'm going to believe in what he's trying to tell me that I need to do better and do differently.
>
> I tried really hard. I might have gotten lazy at some points in the season, but for the most part, taking the season as a whole, I was way more applied to what he was wanting me to do and everything than I'd ever been. I think it really paid off in the relationship. I was committed to him when I told him, "Whatever you ask me to do, I'm going to do it." I offered myself and made myself present and available in case he needed something. I never hung out in the hauler between practices or after practice before. . . . And it was just fun.

The headlines in the 2012 preseason read thus: EARNHARDT JR. WANTS LETARTE TO KEEP STRICT DEMANDS IN PLACE. Which was exactly what I wanted to see.

Dale's attitude reassured me and eliminated any doubts of his commitment. I didn't need to keep pushing him to follow the structure, and that was important. When you gain control, power, and respect, there's a point at which it becomes counterproductive to keep beating your chest and making rules.

I think a lot of bosses and leaders miss this point. If you're the captain of the ship, you set a direction when you leave port, and sometimes you have to be smart enough to just let the journey run its course. Most people keep fiddling with stuff. Occasionally, you've just got to stay hands off.

We were making ground. Dale had his confidence back and was enjoying driving again. With the 2012 season, it would show. Everyone knows it's human nature that if you enjoy doing something, you'll be better at it.

This is hard for people to understand, but racing comes down to a game of inches. If you fire down the backstretch at Kansas Speedway and turn up toward the wall at 206 miles per hour and miss it by six inches, that's two and a half feet by corner entry and six and a half feet by corner exit. By the finish line, you've lost ten and a half feet.

That's why confidence is so critical at two hundred miles per hour.

* * * * *

With Dale's confidence back, the team went to Daytona with way less stress. There were no rule changes, and we were fast all through Speedweeks.

We ended up finishing second in the Daytona 500, and that was a nice shot to start the season.

Two weeks later, it was back to Las Vegas Motor Speedway—the first 1.5-mile speedway of the season and the place where he had made such big gains the year before. There were more 1.5-mile tracks than any other on the schedule, including half the playoffs, so there was some anxiety about this being a big indicator for our season.

We led seventy laps and had a fast Chevrolet. Contact with Mark Martin late in the race on a restart hurt our chances of running well, and we finished tenth.

But it was Dale's postrace comments that defined the state of the team. At times, we had the fastest car but hadn't won. Would he point fingers?

Instead, he stood in front of the media and took the blame for not providing me with the information to fine-tune the setup and stay ahead of the track.

He said we still had to be better.

More importantly, *he* had to do better.

That was a breakthrough. Our turnaround began with the implementation of structure, and it seemed like we were on the right path entering year 2, but you never know until it's tested.

After a disappointing result with such a strong car, Dale could have said, "Well, we didn't stay ahead of this," or "We didn't do this and this and this." But instead, he stood up and held himself accountable. He took responsibility when he could have put blame on anyone else. He was responsible for everything he could control.

The entire team felt that way too and that our biggest spokesman used his chance to say the same—that was huge for morale.

It especially was significant because in past years, Dale always had an excuse in his interviews. There was always a reason that it wasn't his fault.

This time he didn't give any reason other than what he could have done to affect the outcome.

It was what you'd expect to hear from Jimmie Johnson or Matt Kenseth, stand-up champions who lead by example. It was a major step forward.

* * * * *

The season got off to a nice start for us, even though Hendrick Motorsports was struggling as a whole. We were running consistent and better with four top fives in the first thirteen races. It was among the best starts of Dale Jr.'s career.

It started the buzz of. "Well, when is the win going to come?" It was approaching nearly four years since his last victory in the Cup

Series, and now there was reason to believe. You don't win from tenth; you win from running in the top five and leading laps.

That was where the team was heading into Pocono, a triangular 2.5-mile track that I love.

I loved winning there in 2007 with Jeff Gordon in the rain. I love the three unique corners. I love the strategy. I love everything about the track and its long laps and unusual pit maneuvering.

In the June 10, 2012 race, we were just flying. We had by far the best car in the field, and I had us on course with a winning strategy—until the caution flew while we were leading with thirty-five laps remaining. We didn't have enough gasoline to make the finish, but we should have had enough yellows to stretch it. It would have taken a rare occurrence to run out of fuel.

I radioed Dale. "Hey, man, you just need to save gas."

And he started to flip out. "We're going to be short?"

You instantly could hear the fear in his voice that we were going to run him out of gas.

For some reason, I told him, "Well, just come in and pit," basically knowing it would give away the win. It was probably the first time that I didn't make a call that I thought was right. I allowed his fear of failure to overrun the team.

What a dumb, dumb, dumb move I had made.

I could hear in Dale's voice that he wasn't on board with the risk of a poor finish if we ran out of gas. It was the halfway point of the regular season, and we didn't have a win to help ensure we'd make the Chase as a wild card. We finished sixth that day and actually *gained* a spot from third to second in points.

But it was still a dumb move. It was so bad the cars behind ours didn't know *what* to do. "Why is the No. 88 pitting? What are we missing?"

Everyone in the race knew we had put ourselves in position to win—except for Dale.

It was a chess game that we had won before it started. We knew every move our opponent was going to make, and we countered them all. All we had to make was two more moves. And I blew it.

And it reminded me of the importance of setting expectations. It isn't always about having grand plans. Sometimes you have to get down in the mud and map out your scenarios, and we hadn't discussed our plan in prerace. I left that to chance, and that was what I could have done differently. It wasn't an argument or conversation we would be able to have on the radio. It should have been determined well before the race how risky we would be. But the buzz of us being on the verge of a win was real, and you don't want to jinx it by talking about it, so we really didn't have those conversations.

I didn't know where he and I stood on this mentally. If we ran out of gas, would it send him into a tailspin and cause him to lose confidence in the team? Would he bounce back?

I should have been the *leader* of the team. A good leader would have had this discussion ahead of time and prevented it from cropping up out of the blue to wreck our good day.

We had the right car. We had the right strategy. But I wasn't prepared because I didn't have this conversation with my driver. He was supposed to be my biggest teammate.

I could have just fixed it by saying, "No, *this* is what we're doing," and kept him on track and took the calculated risk. Dale might not have been on board, but that was my job. I was in charge of the car.

If I had said, "Stay out," Dale would've driven it to the win. He would have saved enough gas, and all I had to do was tell him.

This was a defining race in all our years together. It's not the races you win that define you, though that's what everybody wants to talk about.

We learned more this day at Pocono than at any race we ever won.

When people talk about the communication between a driver and crew chief, it isn't just "loose" and "tight" handling conditions. We all know that stuff.

It's the emotions. And it's like that in any business.

A great leader can walk through the office and tell whether the staff's having a good day or bad day by the volume of the music being played or the banter and body language between the cubicles or the number of employees at the water cooler. A great leader understands a workforce and team have their own tempo. When it isn't right, you can tell before the results arrive. This was an example of that.

If I had been more prepared as a leader anticipating the tempo, Dale wouldn't have gotten so animated on the radio, and we would have had a more calculated discussion to make a better decision.

All we had worked on Saturday was getting him comfortable driving the car, and all we needed to do to win that race was just talk about the points risks. We didn't even need to go through all the specific scenarios.

Pocono had been repaved, so tire wear wouldn't matter as much as fuel consumption. All we had to do was say, "Hey, Dale, we've been having a good year, and if the window opens right to grab a win, we're going to have to get a little more aggressive to keep our position."

Just a really general conversation. It's like determining within your marriage what's an acceptable amount to spend on a shopping excursion without consulting your spouse. A husband may think buying a flat-screen TV or a set of golf clubs is no big deal, but it may be a purchase his wife will want to discuss.

We needed to establish that threshold at Pocono, and I learned that day this was outside of Dale's comfort zone. I was racing to win races while Dale was concerned about the points and what we would lose if we ran out of gas.

Every exact word I used over the radio mattered. Did I say, "Save a ton?" "Save a little?" "Hey, we're really close?" How did I present it to him, and could I have been better? Maybe it should have been "Hey, man, we're not that far off. We're going to get some yellows. Just save a little bit of gas right here."

So the first mistake was the lack of preparation, and then I compounded it with letting it affect my pit strategy. I should have said, "Hell no! Stay out. We're not pitting." But you have to have the confidence to say that. Easy to say, hard to do.

There are many engineers in NASCAR nowadays who sit next to the crew chief and advise what they should do. It's a whole lot harder to push the radio button yourself to tell the driver. As a crew chief, you press that button, and the whole world sees it.

Luckily, we gave them something better to see the next week.

CHAPTER VIII

My Car Ain't Good

REPAVING A RACETRACK IS LIKE turning real life into a video game.

Michigan International Speedway's two-mile oval was repaved before its June 17, 2012, race, and the result was an ultrasmooth surface that was stupid fast. Marcos Ambrose qualified on the pole at 203.241 miles per hour—the level of speed that normally prompted talk of restrictor plates.

Cars were running 215 miles per hour entering turn 3, and that's a rate at which even superstars (I went through several repaves with Jeff Gordon) can provide very little feedback.

That's why it's like a video game. They still are great drivers, but when they race at Darlington's abrasive surface on old tires, they can drive to the maximum grip of the tire. There's a skill set in a driver's butt, head, and hands that tells them the limit of what the tire will give you.

That doesn't exist in a repave. It's like driving with a joystick where you can tell how far to drive into the corner only by your surroundings, not the feel of the race car. So you just keep going farther into the corner until you almost crash, and then you say, "Okay, I can't go quite that fast."

That's fine in a video game. But this is real life. You can't go until you crash.

So you keep pushing, pushing, pushing until the traction is gone, and then you just hope you can save it. That's what repaves are like. That's why they're so frustrating for a crew chief, because the driver actually is operating *further* from the limit of grip than on a normal track.

On new tires at a worn-out track, drivers operate right to the edge because they can feel it. There's a response. But on fresh pavement, drivers will operate 3 percent away from the edge because they don't know where it is until crossing it.

And when you cross that edge, it hurts—especially at 215 miles per hour.

Dale is a rhythmic, video game–style driver. He isn't as good at qualifying for one lap. What makes him so good at Martinsville are the long eighty-lap, green-flag runs. When he gets into a rhythm, he performs better, and that's why he's so good at running the unique and tricky racing line high up against the wall.

Every driver has a skill set. Dale's isn't driving to the edge of out-of-control; it's that rhythm that takes him to the edge of *performance*. That's what riding the high line around the track is all about.

Jeff Gordon wasn't as good near the wall because his tendency is to overdrive the corner. Most drivers struggle at the top of the track by overdriving it because you literally have to force yourself to lift seconds before you should. It goes against human nature.

Dale is spectacular at that. It's why he is so great on repaved tracks. That's why he was so good a week earlier at the repaved Pocono track, because he could give me lap after lap after lap after lap. The tires don't change on a repave as they do on a worn track, where your handling changes every lap with lost grip.

When you move to the top, you no longer lose grip. You just have to be in that rhythm for lap after lap. Dale can run the top for days, and it's magical to watch.

So a repaved Michigan was right up Dale's alley, just like a repaved Pocono and a repaved Phoenix in 2011 (we were fast there until an untimely caution).

But it still is a struggle for a crew chief because all your typical metrics don't work for setting up the car. Every time you go out on old tires, they go faster.

You can't evaluate anything. It's like trading stocks without the internet. You hope it all works out, but you have no idea of the trends.

We were okay in two practices on Thursday (NASCAR scheduled extra sessions with the new asphalt). There was no hint of a shining light that this would be a special weekend.

On Friday we qualified eighteenth, but we had started to improve the setup and move up the speed chart. We didn't think we had a winning car, but it was turning pretty good. A top-ten car that we figured we could work on in Saturday's final practice and Sunday's race.

And that was when our world—and everyone else's—got turned upside down.

Because the treads were falling apart after fifteen laps at high speed, NASCAR and Goodyear made a last-minute switch Friday night to a new left-side tire that slowed the cars by six miles per hour and stopped the blistering.

NASCAR added a second practice Saturday but didn't relax its rule that allows only one engine per weekend. Our team and many others were already near our self-imposed limits for practice laps to protect against an engine failure during the race.

We were like, "You've got to be kidding me!" We already had scuffed all our tires for the race. Now we had to do it all again across two final practices, and I had hardly any laps left to send out Dale. Hendrick general manager Doug Duchardt and engine tuner Jeff Andrews didn't want me to run him at all.

Mark Martin led the final practice by making fifty-three laps. Dale ran only twenty-six laps before we had to park him.

After the session, our teammate Jimmie Johnson changed engines because of a problem. We searched all over ours, praying we could find a reason to change it because we were way over our lap limit. There was no way this thing would live for four hundred miles Sunday.

My driver, meanwhile, wasn't happy with a practice in which we went from a good, balanced car into a disaster. Our speed was gone, along with my patience, Dale's patience, and the team's. Most of his feedback was complaining instead of informational.

Dale told reporters that the tire, "drove like it's six years old. I'd like to practice more, but I can't. My car ain't as good as I want it, but I can't run any more laps. This ain't cool."

Well, it was about to get worse. Not only would my engine shop and driver be mad at me; it struck the wrong chord with my family too.

* * * * *

The final practice happened after the Xfinity Race, which made it a major inconvenience, because it kept us in the garage for about four hours longer than normal.

The June race at Michigan usually falls on Father's Day week-end, and Motor Racing Outreach, a traveling racetrack ministry, holds a Father's Day Olympics for the families of the drivers, crew chiefs, and team members. My wife, Tricia, and my kids were staying with me that weekend.

The Father's Day Olympics is a family competition that consists of relays, games, nail painting, and other funny, goofy things that the dads do with their kids.

And now I wasn't going to be able to make it, even though it was starting after the last practice. We had to scramble to get the car ready for Sunday. The garage was staying open longer, and as long as it was, I had to be there with my team to work.

So I had to tell my family Friday night that I couldn't be there the next day, which was one more thing weighing on me.

It was like we went from a relaxing vacation at a nice resort to our room not being ready and them losing our luggage.

Everyone was just mad. And then Dale and I had our biggest meltdown ever during the final practice.

He already was angry because he wanted to run more laps and tune the car, and I told him that we had to focus only on scuffing tires because it wouldn't matter how fast we were if we blew a tire.

As a crew chief, sometimes you have to be the dad and send the kids to bed when they want to stay up. You don't want to do that if they're having fun playing Monopoly, but it's your job.

So that was the deal as I made him scuff tires for the race. When we were done with that, he wanted to make a twenty-lap run and figure out what was wrong with the car's handling. "No, Dale. I have Jeff Andrews saying we can't. We're out of laps."

So now Dale was madder than hell that we couldn't go back on the track to improve.

"How are we supposed to get ——ing better if we can't practice?"

"This isn't my decision! It doesn't matter how fast you are if this son of a bitch blows up either! I'm dealing with what is coming my way."

So Dale came flying into the garage stall at one hundred miles per hour, nearly running over people, and threw the steering wheel on the dash as pissy as he could be. As he got out, I tried to stay calm, trying to do the right thing.

"Okay, we'll make a couple of changes and make a couple of laps."

Dale was bitching on his radio the whole way back to the garage from the final run. I climbed down from the roof of the hauler and went right to the lounge to wait for him. He stormed in and started crucifying me.

I told him we needed some time apart, but he just stayed on me. So finally, I snapped.

"You are not ——ing helping the situation! So I'll see you at the debrief."

The Hendrick debrief with all four drivers and crew chiefs was an hour after practice.

Dale kept talking a little bit, and I looked up from my laptop.

"We're ——ing done here. You can go. Matter of fact, you *need* to go. You have a bus. Get out of my trailer. I'll see you at the debrief."

Instantly, you could see by the look on his face that he had no idea what all that meant. I'm normally the jovial guy who never loses his temper. It was kind of like when Rick Hendrick slams his hand down in a meeting—it gets everyone's attention.

Dale had never seen me get to that moment before. It reminded me of making the 2011 Chase at Richmond when Marshall Carlson had to talk me off the cliff. I was at that point again, but Dale wasn't in the car; this time, he was right there with me, and he could see it.

No one was blaming anyone by name, but the actions seemed like people *were* being blamed. The way he was treating me, I reacted to it.

How dare he say this was my fault? We brought a fast race car, and then Goodyear changed the tire. So we had to scuff more tires and couldn't work on the car because of the engine restrictions.

How dare he cuss me up and down about fixing this car? I'd had enough.

When I got to the debriefing, Dale was the first guy there. Doug Duchardt later told me he had arrived ten minutes earlier.

This was where our friendship really helped. We didn't make it personal. He respected me enough, so we sat down and talked and talked and talked. And we learned . . . nothing.

I would love to tell you we solved it, but when we got done, I was no smarter than I was during the middle of our disastrous practice.

The silver lining came when I got back to my bus. TJ Majors, Dale's spotter, had taken my place in the Father's Day Olympics, and he was there hanging with my family and laughing about having his toenails painted pink and his feet painted green with a big 88 painted in black.

TJ had heard I was going to miss the Olympics, so after returning from practice, he went and did all the games, relays, and toenail-painting with my kids. I'm sure he had many other things he wanted to do on a Saturday, but that was the environment we created around our team.

He played along and said, "I'll go do it," because he wanted to take whatever pressure off me that he could. He was the stand-in dad that day for my kids, and they were so thankful. My son actually won the Olympics in his age group with TJ's help.

Top: Ashlyn was no less happy about competing in the Father's Day Olympics with spotter TJ Majors instead of dad. And the following day, I was just as happy. **Credit: Letarte Family Collection**

Right: Being a fill-in for the Father's Day Olympics wasn't a total loss for TJ Majors, who got a painted good luck charm out of it. **Credit: Letarte Family Collection**

Later that night at my bus, my wife, Tricia, could tell something was up and asked what was wrong.

"We're awful. We're going to be lapped at, like, lap 10. We're not even close."

Tricia said she couldn't recall me ever saying something like that before. Usually it was "We're not that bad. We just have to get this a little bit better."

Not this time. There was no sales pitch here.

"We're miserably slow."

"Oh my goodness," she said.

* * * * *

They dropped the green, and we sank like a stone.

But it was because Dale knew the car wasn't great, so he wasn't going to crash it. This is what makes him so special, and sometimes irritating at the same time. He has this calming mind-set that he knows how long four hundred miles is better than anyone.

Dale isn't going to crash the car even if it's handling poorly. Years before, he might have, but now we've built up the accountability side, so he knows that's on him, no matter how badly the car drives. I'd beaten it into his head. "Look, you've just got to get me to the next pit stop so I can work on it. The car does me no good if it's in the fence."

It was like all the things we had built up and worked on were tested over the course of that weekend. We failed one of the tests with that meltdown, but it ended up working out all right.

On the first pit stop, we stuffed a spring rubber in the left rear, and the car settled. And then it was just smart pit strategy. We changed left-side tires only once, and after the mistake at Pocono, we did whatever was necessary to be the leader.

We took the lead from Tony Stewart just past halfway, and then we were gone. We won by 5.3 seconds, an eternity in NASCAR. Dale told me afterward, "I just got out front, and I couldn't see anyone behind me. It was nice and easy."

The whole weekend was surreal. The best moment for a crew chief is when you stand on top of the pit box and watch your team celebrate as the car crosses the finish line.

Those guys on the team are gone as much as I am, but they don't enjoy the same lifestyle—there is no one cleaning their house or pool or yard. I've asked those guys to give and give and give. That is the moment that it makes it all worth it doing what we do.

And that it worked out that I had my family there on Father's Day (and Dale had his wife, Amy, too) made it even more spectacular.

But the odd part looking back was, around the same time, I realized I wasn't long for remaining a crew chief. Racing is like golf in that there are forty competitors, and while Jimmie Johnson may win five races a year, a typical racer wins once or twice a year.

You lose a lot more than you win, and all those weeks in between have to build up for that moment that you have success.

Don't get me wrong, the world rejoiced, and I was happy. I don't think it showed publicly, but privately, I knew that the moment, our first win together and Dale's first in a career-high 143 races wasn't as big as it needed to be. It was a bigger moment for everyone else.

The win didn't move the needle for me as much as it should have. That was when it became clear to me that I wasn't going to be able to do this forever.

All that was wrapped into one race.

Smiles all around just a day after one of the worst fights Dale and I ever had. But we figured out a surprise new tire better than we ever could have expected! **Credit: Harold Hinson Photography**

CHAPTER IX

Lessons

WE SETTLED INTO A NICE summer groove after Michigan, finishing fourth in four of the next nine races and ranking a solid third in points. We were looking good for being championship contenders.

On the last Tuesday and Wednesday in August, I scheduled us for a Goodyear test at Kansas Speedway, which just had been repaved. I picked it because we were so good at Michigan, and I felt we could recreate that magic at Kansas.

We arrived and were head and shoulders the best car there. So on the second day, we made a twenty-five-lap run. I stood on top of the truck and watched Dale keep getting faster and faster—just stupid fast. Fast enough that every other team at the test was pissed.

We just won a couple of months ago by dominating Michigan, and now we were hauling ass again.

And this is why you hate repaves, because it's just so fast and keeps getting faster. By the twentieth lap of that run, I radioed Dale that I needed five more laps. When you reach that length of a run at a test, you're like, "I don't like this. I don't like the speed. I don't like anything about it."

But it's the same feeling you have at every tire test, and it's just part of being a crew chief. You just sit there and count down the laps while hoping for the best.

"Okay, I need three more good ones. Now two more good ones."

Every lap, Dale would make his arc a little bit better, and it took your breath away how fast that place was. And then Dale rolled off into turn 1 wide open, making that big arc to the white line, but then the car turned dead right and hit the fence.

A big hit.

I was standing on top of the hauler in the garage, so I jumped down, hopped in my rental car, and drove right to the scene where the track ambulance had already arrived.

The track's medical staff was great, and Dale already was in the ambulance. I was like, "Hey, man, you all right?"

"Yeah, yeah."

But it was like in slow motion. This was 2012, and people were just beginning to talk about concussions. It might have seemed ignorant now, but we were not doctors and didn't know much about them then.

We brought in the car, and it was narrowed up a *long* way. The other teams at the test were saying, "Holy, shit! You hit a ton." We had another car, and Dale came back after being checked out and asked if we would run it. I told him we had enough and were done. Dale was headed to a Redskins game that night in Washington, DC, anyway.

On our way outside the track, the team stopped at a little barbecue joint, and Dale was quiet. He didn't eat a whole lot, and he later told me he was nauseous. He went to the football game that night, and I texted with him, and he didn't say much about the crash.

We raced Atlanta Motor Speedway that weekend, and I remember driving through the infield tunnel that Friday morning to get to my motorhome before the garage opened, and my phone rang. It was Dale.

"Hey, man, we've got a little problem."

I asked what he meant. He explained the nausea after the hit. Nowadays, that would have triggered alarm bells about concussions, but in 2012, before the awareness of concussions, the reaction was more like, "Well, of course you're hurting, that was a massive hit."

This phone call was another indicator of how my friendship with Dale had progressed and blossomed to the point where I was his first call on a Friday morning when he had some big questions.

He trusted me to help him navigate the situation, just like a quarterback would tell a head coach that his shoulder was bothering him even if he looked fine in practice during the week. *Let's work this out before the game begins.*

Dale asked if we had a backup driver just in case for Atlanta.

"I can do the race, but if I need some help and my body needs rest. What's our plan? I'm sure I'll be fine, but I felt I should call you just in case."

Timeout, I said.

"Have you talked to Rick?"

"No. That's why I'm calling you."

I told him we needed to run it by Rick because I couldn't hire backup drivers on my own.

"Look, man, I've got your back, but that's over my pay scale."

I started by calling Jesse Essex, the PR director at Hendrick Motorsports. Jesse always has steered me in the right direction and has a unique personality for staying calm in the worst situations—and he unfortunately has too much experience with that.

As Rick likes to joke, you can't lie to your lawyer, your accountant, or your PR guy, and that was why I called Jesse first. He recommended I call Rick.

"All right," Rick said. "What do you think we should do?"

I told him we needed to figure out if we would have a driver. Rick had a thought.

"If Dale can't do it, just park it."

Practice was in about six hours. Rick had some names, but they would need approval from Chevrolet and sponsors. So he said if Dale couldn't drive, we would put the No. 88 on jack stands and wouldn't qualify. He still was locked into the race.

If necessary, Dale would take the night off and relax, healing up after being left sore by such a massive hit in Kansas.

If that happened, Rick said I should let him know so that he could call NASCAR president Mike Helton and our sponsors before the news went public. He wanted them to learn from him instead of the media.

"We'll make the statement that it's Dale Jr.'s car and until he gets back, we're not just going to throw someone in it. We'll start last."

So I called Dale with our plan, and he was good with it.

When practice arrived, Dale decided he could drive and was 36th fastest. I stuck my head in the car to ask what Dale needed to be better.

"I have no idea."

* * * * *

Our team was never known for its qualifying speed, so I was unsure whether our car's handling was just that bad or our driver still was feeling the lingering effects of a massive hit.

We had to trudge through and push forward. Being the leader of the team and making the key decisions, I decided that a car that is guaranteed to be tight—meaning, it goes a little straighter with the front tires and is more secure—is a little easier for drivers to handle the majority of the time. They usually slide a little bit, get out of the gas, and can recover.

So I hedged my bets and pointed the car in that direction to make sure that was how it drove. Dale qualified thirty-fifth and was twentieth in final practice. We weren't making improvements, and frustration was setting in with the race team.

But we kept our heads down and strategically worked through the weekend. Real life is about having good days and bad days. Sometimes, you just don't have it—what's the plan to get through that? We approached the situation with Dale with "Let's get the best we can out of what we have" without begin affected by disappointments or expectations.

Dale was awful to start the race; he just was trying to stay out of the way. But he got back on the lead lap through a caution with fifty laps remaining, and the car came to him.

"Stevie, just get it dialed back in, and I'll get to the front." We went all the way back, making significant changes on the last stop. My team guys were telling me, "Dude, we're going to crash."

"It'll be fine."

Dale went from twenty-second to seventh on the final run. It was like a hobbled quarterback leading his team on a winning touchdown drive.

The next week was Richmond, and Dale said he felt way better. He won the pole position even though we weren't that fast in practice. We made all these changes before qualifying, and Dale shot straight to the top, and I thought that was it.

The guy had to be healed, right? He was fixed. He qualified first a week after struggling to eat because he was so nauseous. Everything must be okay.

We started the playoffs with three average showings, and then all hell broke loose on the last lap at Talladega Superspeedway.

* * * * *

Tony Stewart threw a block while leading in the final corner of the race at Talladega, starting a twenty-six-car crash that involved Dale Jr. Though he ranted about restrictor-plate racing afterward, Dale didn't seem that hurt—he actually gave Jimmie Johnson a ride back to the garage from the pits.

But Dale's head was snapped around in the crash, and he called me on Tuesday morning, saying he didn't feel good again. We immediately got Rick involved and went to see Dr. Jerry Petty, a Charlotte neurologist who works with many drivers.

During this process, Rick never asked once about whether Dale could race again or when; the only thing he was concerned about was his driver's well-being. His empathy for Dale Jr. was all about being a good person and a friend.

We made the decision that Dale didn't need to be driving, but we couldn't tell anybody for a couple of days until Thursday, when the garage was opening at Charlotte Motor Speedway.

Rick also determined Dale's replacement would be Regan Smith, who was driving for James Finch. I asked Rick if we were going to ask Finch for permission.

"Nope," Rick said. "We're not going to talk to anybody. I'll line up Finch's backup driver."

Finch was getting chassis and engines from Rick, and they had a business relationship in which Rick just knew he could make this change without talking to Finch.

So that was what we did. On Thursday morning at seven, shortly before the release went out that Dale Jr. was out of the car, I texted Regan: "Hey, man, are you up? This is Steve Letarte. We need to talk about something." He texted right back: "I'm up now."

I told him the situation that he was going to drive the No. 88 that weekend for Dale. Regan thought he had to call Finch. I told him Rick already had. The decision was made.

I told Regan to meet me at Hendrick so we could get him fitted for a seat. We already had loaded the car with Dale's stuff and sent it to Charlotte, knowing it would be a pain to replace it, but we couldn't have anyone knowing.

I called Adam Jordan, the interior mechanic on Dale's car, just after calling Regan and told him he had to be at the shop ASAP. We all met at Hendrick and started putting in Jimmie Johnson's seat liner, which Regan liked better. Then we headed to the track to change over Dale's car and do the news conference to announce Dale Jr. was out.

There wasn't much for my boss, driver or me to be happy about the morning we announced a concussion took Dale out of the seat at Charlotte. **Credit: Harold Hinson Photography**

The prognosis for Dale's recovery was to sit in a dark, quiet room, so we didn't see him that weekend, though he did begin to text me during the race.

Regan qualified twenty-sixth and finished thirty-eighth. We were running pretty well near the start and passing Kyle Busch for a top-five spot when the difference became apparent. If it were Dale Jr., the pass would have been completed, because of Busch's respect for a veteran peer.

But as Kyle pulled down while Regan went by on the outside, he realized, "Wait, that isn't Dale." And he rolled right back onto our quarter-panel, so up the track we went and lost a spot.

Regan was like "What the hell?"

And we told him, "Look, no one is going to like you passing them. We're thirty laps in, so let's just ride."

We pitted, put on tires, went back out and the engine blew up. We ran hot under yellow, and the gauges began to flash, and we hadn't gone over how to handle that. We were out of time. Dale would have seen the gauges and understood what to do.

I wish we could have run that race again, because we would have finished top ten. (There was some measure of redemption a month later at Homestead-Miami Speedway, where I called the strategy for Regan's JR Motorsports debut, and we won the Xfinity Race.)

Back in the No. 88, Regan went to Kansas, where the testing wreck had happened that initially had given Dale a concussion. It was stupid fast because of the repave, and Regan had a terrific save in qualifying to keep it off the wall (Dale texted later and joked, "See, I'm not the only one who can't qualify that piece of shit!")

Regan started thirty-ninth and finished a respectable seventh—and then Dale came back at Martinsville Speedway.

Hendrick Motorsports has enjoyed unbelievable success at Martinsville with a team-record twenty-four victories (nine apiece by Jeff Gordon and Jimmie Johnson). It's the tightest, slowest track on the NASCAR circuit, a half-mile with top speeds barely more than one hundred miles per hour.

While there's a tremendous amount of beating and banging, it's at much slower, more cautious speeds that made the track the perfect place for Dale's return.

And the weekend went well: Dale qualified twentieth and ran into the top ten for much of the race. He was running seventh with twenty-five laps remaining when the caution flew, and I made a really aggressive pit call to try to win the race.

Instead of pitting, I kept Dale on the track on old tires, putting him in second behind Brad Keselowski for a restart with nineteen laps to go. He tentatively drove it like a little kid, got run up the track, and crashed ten laps later.

Afterward, I was mad, and he was mad. I was like, "Dude, what happened? Did it drive that bad?"

And he said, "All I wanted to do was ——ing finish."

And that was when it sank in that I had come there to win the race but he hadn't.

This was a conversation about expectations that we should have had but didn't. What was our goal here? In my mind, it was to win. In his, it was to return from injury.

Going through these things together was what made Dale and me closer than anything we probably did on the track. The 2012 season was as much of a roller coaster as any I had had.

When you look at the disappointments we weathered at Pocono and Michigan (before our win), you realize sometimes losing is more important to building a team than winning. I think it's something we've got to learn in our country too. Everybody can get along in times of greatness, but it's the tough times that shape people and make relationships—and teams—better.

Another thing I learned is that winning isn't enough to offset the rest in life. The 2012 season with Dale's concussion and the 2007 season, when I came as close to a championship as I ever would with Jeff Gordon, molded me more than any other years.

I learned more about being a leader working with Dale than in five seasons with Jeff, because he was so good at being a leader.

That's not a knock on working with Jeff. People can't understand how much he accomplishes and whom he surrounds himself with to be so great. The well-oiled machine that is Jeff Gordon is so smooth you don't even realize how good you have it while you're a part of it. My learning curve naturally slowed with him.

With Dale, it was the opposite—the learning was accelerated, and whoever was my second driver as a crew chief, I was going to be so much better with them. So Dale and I outran the expectations, while Jeff and I probably didn't reach them.

But if Dale had been first, I don't know if I'd have made it. Whoever was getting the second half of my crew chief career was going to get the better years.

Dale and I are close—I was at his wedding, we text—in a way that Jeff and I never have been. My friendship with Jeff was never like being buddies. It was a mentor-student dynamic.

So the 2012 season had me reflecting on a lot of things personally and professionally, the ups and downs in racing. It sort of felt like when you get sick and know something's wrong but you don't know what it is.

Dale's win at Michigan was a highlight to the world, and it had the fans and NASCAR rejoicing. It was a big deal, but it didn't move my needle nearly as much as it probably should have.

I didn't want to admit it. And I couldn't tell Dale, because what purpose would it serve when it was something that meant the world to him to win again?

But at the end of 2012, I did have a conversation with Dale. "Hey, I'm not going to do this forever." Because we had a lot of conversations about how long he wanted to do it too and maybe we could get our careers to line up.

By the conclusion of our second season together, I could see our careers weren't going to line up. I had the conversation with him and the team that I wanted to have a plan for how I eventually would leave the team. I didn't know when that would be or how we'd choose a successor, but I wanted to have that conversation and discuss expectations in a way that we hadn't before the race at Martinsville.

It was time for me to look beyond being Dale's crew chief.

CHAPTER X

Subconscious Commitment

THE 2013 SEASON WAS JUST kind of odd. The expectations were diminished because of the concussion—we were ranked ninth in preseason projections, which was realistic.

We finished second in the Daytona 500 (for the second straight year) to Jimmie Johnson, won a couple of pole positions, and finished fifth in the points standings. There wasn't anything magical about it.

We were good enough to make the playoffs on points and not good enough to do anything more. The best race might have been Michigan, where Dale returned to the site of his most recent win and was leading when his engine failed.

That was the type of season it was.

It also was the type of season I couldn't have had with Dale in our first year together. It showed we had settled into a groove of being able to muddle through, despite occasionally having average cars, and yet still finish top five in points. We broke another engine in the opener of the playoffs, killing our championship hopes, and then went on a tear in which we finished top ten in eight of the last nine races.

At Dover, we sat on the pole with the best car and four tires on the final stop, and yet we lost to Jimmie, who had two tires. If it were anyone other than Jimmie Johnson, the greatest driver in Dover history, we would have won that race. That one hurt.

At Talladega, we had the race won with Dale guaranteed to pass Jamie McMurray for the lead in the final corner . . . when the caution came out. We finished second again.

So it was that kind of season with near misses that were no one's fault. We had good cars and bad. We had races that were frustrating and good. It was a year of average performances. Nothing ever fell in our lap to make us better. And we had five runner-up finishes, finishing right behind our teammate Jimmie at Daytona, Texas, and Dover.

I know it sounds odd, but the first half of the year, there really were no memorable moments. It wasn't good or bad; it just didn't match the intensity of 2012 and returning Dale to victory lane for the first time in four years.

What I remember most about 2013 is the second half of the season and all the soul-searching over my internal decision to leave or stay at Hendrick. In my mind, that's what I remember about that year.

I had worked at Hendrick Motorsports since I was sixteen, and I was thirty-four. It was the only job I'd ever had for nearly two decades. I'd driven to work in that building a few thousand times, and it was my entire identity. I've known people longer at Hendrick than I've known my wife—by a lot.

It was kind of like I had to divorce one family to spend time with my other family. That was what made it so difficult. And there was a chain of events that happened throughout 2013 that cleared the way toward it becoming the right path.

If we win instead of finishing second those five times, do I remain a crew chief? If the engine doesn't blow at Michigan, do I still wind up doing TV?

You can plan and prepare for life as much as you want, but you have to accept things as they come, and that was what this decision was about. There are a few hundred things that could have changed the course of what led to me being at NBC.

If I hadn't had an offhand conversation with a pit reporter. If I hadn't volunteered to work for ESPN in their on-camera garage as a younger guy. If I hadn't done a weekly spot on SiriusXM Satellite Radio as Dale's crew chief.

I had no idea any of that would be résumé fodder for a career in media while I was doing it, but that was what happened. When I sat down with NBC, they knew everything I had done.

Life isn't always blueprinted.

Those people who have such an ink-on-paper view of their lives, career, and future that include two kids, a dog, and a white picket fence—all that does is often set you up for disappointment. You have to let things play out. You may not be able to dream big enough to know where life can take you.

You need to be an active participant in a life where you don't know what's coming next. That's the key. You can't be a passenger.

It's okay to plan, but it's also okay when plans don't end up as you think they will.

It made a difference that it was NBC getting back into NASCAR. If it had been Fox or ESPN retooling, I might have passed, because I figured they'd be back with another offer in a few years. But this was a chance to get in on the bottom floor of a new era of NASCAR TV.

I still probably made a list of twenty pros and cons about whether to leave Hendrick, where I could have stayed the rest of my life. My wife, Tricia, was my strongest supporter. She allowed me to make the decision without any family pressure. When I eventually made the decision to leave, it was because I wanted to spend time with my kids, not because it was necessary or because anyone asked for it. It was because I wanted to make a change.

And while the dance recitals and birthday parties are popular to talk about as the things you don't want to miss, it really was taking my kids to school every day that meant the most to me. It's the time you get to spend with them, not the moments you share.

If you're a super busy person who is trying just to be there for the moments without being mentally there, you really aren't there anyway. I enjoy the days of nothingness with my family. My joy today is our going to put the football game on or play cards or argue about whatever. That time with them is as important as any prear- ranged or scheduled moment.

There weren't any moments on the track that led to this decision. My family was, without a doubt, the primary reason.

Everything I had sacrificed to reach this point in my life finally added up. It's like a five-gallon bucket that isn't heavy as you begin to throw change in it. But somewhere around the five millionth penny, you can't lift it anymore.

I missed a lot of things in high school (I didn't even walk across the stage at graduation because I was racing). I didn't go to college (despite numerous scholarship offers). I'm not ungrateful or complaining about those decisions, but right then I felt I had the power to choose.

I had watched coworkers die at forty-five from cancer. I wanted to spend time with my kids while they were young, and selfishly, I wanted time for me while I was still healthy. Racing opened doors for me that I never could have walked through, and I don't take any of that for granted.

Here's the best way to explain it: From my late teens to when I was thirty-five, there had been more than two hundred summer weekends in my adult life, and I'd been working for all but maybe fifteen of them.

Think about that the next time you're watching your favorite baseball team. You have no idea what they've sacrificed to get there. I was fortunate enough to sit in the owner's box for my favorite team, the Boston Red Sox, but that wasn't handed to me. I had to give up a lot to enjoy that once-in-a-lifetime experience, and when it was over, it was back to the grind.

What I really wanted was just some normalcy in my life.

You can't have it all. I was willing to give up flying around with Dale Jr. in his jet to go hang out in Key West. I was ready to trade that for normalcy. Now I go to Harris Teeter every Monday morning after I drop my kids off at school, and I do our grocery shopping for the week. And I love it.

I'm thirty-eight, and I never have done a load of laundry in my life because I spent most of it on the road for 220 days a year. The things that people may not love to do that they take for granted, some of those things I love to do.

90

When Carl Edwards announced he was stepping away for the 2017 season, he said something that struck a chord about the commitment needed to compete at the highest level. It's a subconscious commitment.

My wife jokes about it, but I think deep down it crushes her when she recalls the times in my life when I can tell you the front springs we've run at Charlotte but I can't tell you a single name of a kid in my daughter's classes.

People are like computers—there is only so much RAM we have for storage. I've worked alongside Chad Knaus, the best crew chief ever to set foot in the garage, and it's because racing is the number 1 thing in his life. He doesn't have kids. He doesn't talk to his family. Nothing is more important than racing.

Chad was at a level that I was able to work next to, and that drove me into retirement because I knew I never could beat his commitment. There was no possible way.

My quote from a 2014 *USA Today Sports* story about Chad and his No. 48 team's success with Jimmie Johnson sums it up:

> *I ask myself did I leave crew chiefing because I couldn't balance it or because I see how successful Chad is not needing to (balance it)? Is that why I left? Everybody says, "What's the 48's secret?" Well, I see them. I know every secret. I know every setup. I've seen the dynasty grow. You'd be silly not to make that the template for success. There has to be a point where I question if that's what I based my decision on. I'm a crew chief in the sport and choosing not to be. And I love my job and everything about it, but I see what he gives to be successful.*
>
> *There's no extra time. He gives 100% of his effort to his company. If any effort goes anywhere else, he's going to have to give less. That's not a knock on anyone. But he doesn't make any decisions for any reason other than success. So when you have any sort of other requirements, whether personal, profes-*

sional or family or whatever they might be, I don't see how he has room for anything else the way he currently does it.

I knew I couldn't do it as well and be as committed as Chad. He has a wife now, and I hope he is willing to be 80 percent as good, but that's his business, right? I don't spend as much time with him anymore, but I've seen it.

So that was what was going through my head while I weighed the decision to leave or stay at Hendrick in 2013.

I didn't get burned out as a crew chief because of anything Rick Hendrick or his top lieutenants, Doug Duchardt and Ken Howes, expected of me. I talk to Rick Hendrick more now than I did as a crew chief, because he didn't have time to manage us. He would check in and always make sure we knew that if we needed anything, he would help.

I got burned out because that's how it works. Externally, I never could appear to be having a bad day as a crew chief. My personality masked a lot of what bothered me, but internally, I was managing all that, and it was exhausting.

That ages you.

And it's your entire identity. I've been gone more than two years, and I still run into people who think I'm a crew chief at Hendrick. I wanted to prove to myself that I could survive outside the make-believe world where I loved to work for nearly twenty years.

I wanted to build a legacy of my own and a brand in which I could claim ownership that didn't say I was a Hendrick employee. When I'm seventy-five, I want my legacy to be multichaptered.

* * * * *

At the October 2013 race at Charlotte Motor Speedway, Dale said, "Hey, man, I got to talk to you."

"Yeah, man, what's up?"

"Rick said you might be going to work for TV."

We finished fifteenth that night—our only finish outside the top ten after the blown engine at Chicagoland.

My phone rang just as I walked out of the drivers' meeting, and it was Rick.

"Hey, man, I messed up."

"Oh, I know," I told him.

As sharp as Rick is, sometimes he misspeaks. He had been talking to Dale about something, and he casually mentioned that I'd been in talks with NBC, and then he realized that Dale had no idea.

So we didn't run well at Charlotte because of it, and that just proved we were like brothers. It wasn't that he was upset I was leaving; it was that he didn't want to hear it from someone else. That was a big deal.

So I went to Dale's motorhome before the race, and we talked it out. For a guy who many believe lives in his own world, Dale is the most unselfish person I've ever met. He was going to be a huge part of my choice.

By the season finale at Homestead-Miami Speedway a month later, I'd made my decision. I told Dale I was going to take the NBC deal.

After Jimmie Johnson won the championship, I went by Dale's motorhome (he was staying over to drive to Key West the next day), and we talked for an hour.

"Listen, as a race car driver, I don't want you to go," Dale told me. "I love working with you. But, man, you're going to be great. You'll be awesome! You should do it."

I'm not as close to Dale as others—his spotter, TJ Majors, was his best man—but he's one of my confidantes. He's somebody whom I would lean on, and in one of the biggest decisions of my life, he approved.

We got the deal done to start in 2015—meaning, I would return for a last season with Dale in 2014—and I didn't tell anybody about it until we were planning to announce it at preseason testing at Daytona in early January.

We were going to tell the team at dinner after the first day of the test and then announce the news the next day. I was standing next to my hauler when my phone rang, and I didn't recognize the number. I answered, and it was Dave Moody of the Motor Racing Network.

Basically, he was planning to post our news on his blog and discuss it on his SiriusXM show that afternoon but wanted to give me a chance to comment first.

A brief flashback to Chicagoland Speedway the previous September, where Jeff Burton pulled me aside in the motorhome lot. We talked a lot, but it usually was a lot of "Hey, man, are you fighting the bump in turn 1 too?" Not this time.

"Hey, are you talking to NBC?"

NBC Sports Group had begun talking to me in early October, two days after my non negotiation clause had expired with Hendrick (allowing me to explore other options). I had dinner at Morton's with several of the network's executives, and Tricia, who is an attorney and who agreed to be my agent, began negotiating on a potential deal while I mulled whether to leave crew-chiefing.

"Yes, I'm talking to NBC. Why do you ask?"

"Because I'm talking to them too."

We went into Burton's motorhome for five minutes, and he told me that NBC Sports Group executive producer and president of production, Sam Flood, told him they were looking to hire a big-name crew chief and that it would be a great booth combination. Eventually, my name came up. Burton said he hadn't told anybody else.

"I hated racing against you because you're real creative on top of the pit box and your strategies would piss me off. But this is going to be great. We're going to be great."

I told him I hadn't made a decision yet, and he said he just wanted me to know that he was committed to doing it.

"I think you'd be great at it, and I just wanted to let you know that I'm going to work as hard at that as I've worked at driving."

We talked about the possibility here and there after that, and he mentioned that he heard our play-by-play announcer would be Rick Allen.

Flash-forward again to the 2014 test at Daytona, where I hung up with Dave Moody, walked out of the back of my hauler . . . and there was Rick Allen, who had been announced as the new play-by-play announcer for NASCAR on NBC a month earlier.

We were making small talk, and then here came the media, taking photos and waiting around. Moody's story had broken, and now I was outside the back of my hauler, talking to a future TV coworker, without having told anyone on my team about the news.

Laura Scott, the No. 88 PR representative, came out of the hauler and suggested that (a) I stop talking to Rick Allen and (b) I come back inside the truck.

* * * * *

I called an emergency meeting with my guys to explain what was happening. This was extremely difficult because I'd known many of the No. 88 team members for so long.

Jason Burdett, my car chief, was one of my best friends and the best man at my wedding. I virtually had raised Jason Seitzinger, the team's shock specialist, who was hired as an eighteen-year-old kid by former crew chief Robbie Loomis.

Adam Jordan also was someone I'd hired very young and cultivated through the system. TJ Majors did the Father's Day Olympics with my kids the day before Dale's breakthrough win at Michigan.

Every one of these guys had carried my sleeping daughter to our car at some point after a flight home from a long race weekend. Now I had to tell them, "Hey, I'm bailing. Good luck."

As I explained it, I was getting choked up and looking for words. I couldn't get anything out, and that was when Dale Jr. saved me and was spectacular.

"Look, guys, I've been talking to him about this since last season. We knew he wasn't going to crew-chief forever. He's a good guy."

In that Dale Jr. sort of way, he bailed me out of the moment, which was among the most awkward of my life. The last thing I wanted was for the guys to hear it from the media.

They all thought something was wrong because I interrupted testing and pulled TJ off the spotter's stand to hold the meeting. "Oh, shit, what did we forget? Stevie must be pissed about something."

I apologized they had to hear it that way, but they were crushed. We're a pack of traveling gypsies, and I wear everything on my sleeve. I'm not a reserved, private guy. That's not me. Everybody's been to my house. Their kids have swum in the pool with my kids. Birthdays, baptisms—I've done them all.

Some of them took it personally. Some got quiet, some walked out, and some couldn't look me in the eye.

We went to dinner that night, and then I lay in bed awake in my hotel room, thinking about the press conference the next day with Sam Flood and Jeff Burton.

NBC Sports Group executive producer and president of production Sam Flood had a good feeling about pairing me with Jeff Burton.
Credit: Motorsport Images/Eric Gilbert

Tricia and I talked about the potential questions I'd hear about why I was leaving, and I said I'd just be honest and explain I was exhausted in some ways and wanted a more normal life with my family. Playing the role of PR person, Tricia said that would resonate well, especially because it was real.

I didn't want any of it to sound like excuses; I just wanted to stick with answers that everyone related to that were 100 percent factual. When my little girl made her first Communion, I was in Kansas. That stays with you.

I think the message was well-received, and I don't think anybody was negative about my reasons for doing it.

But then the focus turned to how things would go in my final year with Dale. Typically, lame-duck seasons fare poorly.

The question came from another future coworker, Nate Ryan, who then was working at *USA Today Sports*.

"This is a unique situation, having a crew chief that has a known expiration date, but it's not so unique for drivers," Nate said. "Oftentimes, when you have a lame-duck driver, it doesn't lead to great results and devolves into a morass of ill will and hurt feelings and poor performance—"

I jokingly interrupted, "That's a good pep talk. I'll tell you what, I think we should break on that one!"

Nate followed up with, "How is it going to be different from a crew chief perspective knowing this is it, this is one and done, and you guys still want to win a championship? How are you guys still going to deliver that high level? Maybe part of the answer is that you guys ended last year on such a high note. Is that almost beneficial that this last season is coming after your best season so far with the 88?"

As I told Tricia I would respond, I simply was honest. "I think what makes this situation unique compared to any driver situation I can remember is that I'm not going to crew-chief for another organization, so when I go to Charlotte with Dale Jr., it's going to be our last trip together to Charlotte, and I feel I have the best job in the garage area. I've enjoyed every race we've run together, every practice we've run together. The best parts of my job are the four hours on Sunday afternoon we try to go win.

"So I think that this is a very different situation, because I'm not working on being a broadcaster in 2014, I'm working on filling a trophy case, and to do that we have to win our first race. Dale and I have had that conversation, and he said it the best, that this will give us an opportunity to really cherish those races and those opportunities, and I think, if anything, it might allow us to be better at our jobs, because frustration sets in for everyone in the garage area. It's a tough sport. If it doesn't set in, you don't care enough about your job.

"And I think this is one more thing that could maybe drag us out of frustration, because you know, there's a time stamp on the end of it. So do you really want to throw away your last trip to Sonoma together? Do you want to put personal feelings in the way of trying to win the Brickyard? I think to do that would really . . . it would be a shame for what we've built over the last three years, and I don't think it would happen. I think social media, and perhaps the media, would have more of an issue with it than we would internally on the race team."

It was a good answer, but what I left out of it was that I was scared to death about the question.

I was worried about 2014 not just because it was going to be my last season as a crew chief but because I couldn't explain why we didn't win in 2013.

So how the hell can I tell you we're going to win in 2014?

It was a scary question to face. Thankfully, we quickly answered it.

CHAPTER XI

$1,479

WINNING THE 2014 DAYTONA 500 was the biggest moment of my professional life, and that only continues to grow and be redefined every year.

You'd think the significance of that race would have been clear when I watched my car cross the finish line . . . when I walked into victory lane . . . when I was honored the next morning with my team at the champion's breakfast.

That should have been enough to appreciate the magnitude of our victory, but it never really began to hit me until weeks later—maybe months—and I'm reminded more of its bearing with each passing day.

In my crew chief career—330 races, 15 victories, 112 top fives, and 185 top tens—it's hard to reflect on every decision I made, every race I won and every race I lost. As they become more distant in time, those moments diminish in meaning.

The Daytona 500 is the complete opposite.

Every decision I made in 2014 to win the Great American Race is more impactful now than ever. When I'm introduced now, it's as Daytona 500–winning crew chief. Every day, that victory becomes more important than it was a week after, a month after, a year after. More than four years later, it's more important than it's ever been.

It's a constant reminder that of all the decisions we make in life, sometimes the ones that seem the most monumental aren't in retrospect.

Of all the things I've agonized and sweated over, the 2014 Daytona 500 victory is the most momentous thing I've done.

Even though it hardly seemed that way in the weeks leading up to it. Throughout my life, I've dreamed about winning the Daytona 500, and I was lucky to do it three times with Jeff Gordon. There have been seasons in which the anticipation of winning the biggest race of the season felt palpable—the team flies down in February with fresh luggage and uniforms, just raring to go.

But after wrestling with the emotions of an off-season in which I had revealed it would be my last year with Dale, I don't remember dreaming we would win the race until we did. Subconsciously, I never got there because my brain was swimming with other emotions; I didn't have time to stop and say, "We're here to win the Great American Race."

This actually was a good thing, because it meant there were no distractions from being focused on the task at hand.

Of course, Dale is always good on restrictor-plate tracks—we had finished second the past two years in the Daytona 500. He talked with such reverence about superspeedway racing, while most people hate going because of the big wrecks and the lack of control in your on-track fate.

But the whole week leading up to our race felt normal. I don't know whether it was the nerves of my final Daytona 500 with Dale or the peace in having made the decision. But nothing stood out about that Speedweeks aside from our car consistently being good.

It felt right to be in the routine of working again after the chaos of the off-season. The at-track regimens and practice schedules that I'd implemented through the first three seasons with Dale paid off, and we didn't even need to practice Saturday, the day before the race.

Two days before on Friday night, Tricia and I took our kids to dinner, and we got a call from Doug Yates's wife, Whitney, on the way back to come check out their motorhome. We did, along with many glasses of wine, and we ended up riding around the infield until one in the morning, hanging out with the fans.

I was hanging loose because there was no reason to practice Saturday. We were that good. That feeling carried over to the race, which was paused by a six-hour delay for rain after the first thirty-eighth laps. I just sat in the motorhome with my wife and kids and played cards while my brother-in-law went out to get us chicken wings. Dale and his family passed the time by playing Scrabble.

Before that, Dale and I just hung out atop the pit box for an hour, waiting for the deluge of rain to stop.

It was special. We had Dale's sister Kelley up there with us during the race too.

It was another example of how some of NASCAR's best moments are extraordinarily well-timed—the fight on the backstretch to end the 1979 Daytona 500, the first shown on national TV. . . Richard Petty's two hundredth win at Daytona when President Ronald Reagan was in attendance.

Dale Jr. had been at the center of some of these. He won the first race at Daytona after his father's death, the first race after September 11, the Daytona 500 in 2004, which marked the debut of a new title sponsor.

And now here was another win in the Daytona 500, the first race after announcing that I would be leaving his team.

I'm a believer that those moments are what makes sports great, because it really happens across all of sports if you just are a fan. I try to tell people to have just a little bit of childhood belief in greatness. Believe that anything can happen. Not enough people hold on to this anymore. Too many are cynical or look at everything negatively.

I'm the opposite. I was raised to believe if I have a bad day or more than two in a row, I should change things. When my family flies across the country, I tell my son to look out the window and realize there are 325 million people out there. So don't let people tell you that you can't do anything.

On the flight home from my biggest win, Tyler sported a Daytona 500 champion's hat – evidence of the greatness I teach him to strive to find.
Credit: Letarte Family Collection

Some things are harder than others, some things don't fit your style, but you have to be able to believe there are greater things. That was how I got through my career, because if you only let the NASCAR garage be your world, I don't know how you would make it.

So we won the biggest race of the year. We didn't back into it. In our last attempt together, Dale and I went out and won it. He led the final eighteen laps and held off Brad Keselowski in a final restart shootout—that's the moment everyone remembers, but I knew even earlier that he would win.

When Dale has the right car at Daytona, he can do what he wants with it. There was a point with about twenty-five laps to go when we were shuffled out of the lead and hung on the outside by ourselves, and he still managed to keep us in second by side-drafting.

That was the moment when I knew we would win the Great American Race.

The question of if we could win in our last season together was answered quickly in a Daytona 500 victory. **Credit: Letarte Family Collection**

Between telling the team at the test in January and the race in February, there had been many lunches and cups of coffee at the shop in Charlotte over those weeks to explain my move to the guys.

I realized what made it hard for some was the same reason that made it great: I had a relationship with all of them, and it meant different things to each, so I couldn't cover it all in a meeting. I had to spend time with each and let everyone ask what they wanted to know. They deserved more than that, but that was what I could give them.

By the time we went to Daytona in February, we were all good. And then we won. It was beyond anything I could have dreamed. The magnitude of what we accomplished really didn't sink in until years later.

But there were some great memories from the celebration that night too. Ending the biggest race of the season in prime time was incredible. Having the guys all jump over the wall and the confetti flying in victory lane under the lights—it was a special kind of blur.

Tricia brought the kids to the celebration in their pajamas. We have a great shot of my little girl waking up with a big smile from sleeping on my shoulder just as the photo was snapped. I have another photo that I love of my son wearing his team hat at the end of the night.

The race ended so late we didn't celebrate too long because we had to be in bed to wake up early a few hours later to enshrine our winning car at Daytona USA and get our rings and leather jackets as the winners.

This was after we tore down the car for NASCAR's postrace inspection and then put it back together for the morning's festivities. When I got done with my media center interviews, the crew still was outside, finishing that work. I went over to my motorhome to bring a case of beer and found I was all out, so I "borrowed" a cooler of beer from the Ford hospitality motorhome (thinking back, I still might owe them a cooler).

As we reassembled the No. 88 car for the winner's ceremony, everyone finished off our competition's beer (I figured Ford would get over it after we'd beat them).

There were hundreds of text messages, but I remember one in particular as we were getting on the Hendrick plane to head home. There's a Mexican restaurant in Martinsville called Mi Ranchito that we always go to while in town. The manager has been there forever, and he always holds a table for the team and me.

As we were leaving Daytona, and everyone was exhausted, a text message popped up with a 256 area code. The Mi Ranchito manager wanted to tell everyone congratulations. I was like, "Guys! Guys! Look who texted us!"

The plane erupted with cheers.

* * * * *

The only downside to the Daytona celebration was, the team didn't get much time with Dale because he was whisked away Monday morning for a media tour in New York.

Dale had a plan, though. Knowing the team would be staying out west between the Phoenix and Las Vegas races the next two weeks, he suggested getting together for an all-day celebration of the win in Vegas.

One of our team members had a connection to the Margaritaville restaurant and bar on the Strip across from the Bellagio. We rented out the top floor as a private party and took the moment to truly celebrate as a team over the course of several hours.

We started around 1:00 p.m. and hung out until long after the sunset. There were maybe fifteen of us, and I've still got a photo of the receipt from the bar tab: $1,479. The only food order was a couple of baskets of chips and salsa. We went through about two-dozen buckets of beer, but it wasn't as if this was a crazy night of getting drunk—it was just a great time.

Just to prove there was no embellishment of our Las Vegas victory party ($10.49 for chips and dip? You've got to be kidding me!). **Credit: Letarte Family Collection**

There was no ticker tape parade. No public celebration with loud music and fireworks. It was a bunch of good friends and teammates sitting around laughing, joking, and drinking beer for several hours.

It felt like the first time we had gotten back into our rhythm since I'd made the announcement two months earlier that it would be my last season as crew chief. All these guys whom I felt I had helped raise in NASCAR just enjoying one another's company.

There were a few other poignant moments from the aftermath of the victory. Dale made his official debut on Twitter, and his second tweet was a picture of him standing in front of his father's statue outside the track.

And many remember that I told Dale "I love you, man, I love you" in response to his "Hell, yeah!" after taking the checkered flag.

Even though I don't remember it.

What I've learned about those moments in racing is that you can't slow them down. I can't remember anything that was said in the five minutes after that race. I remember Kelley Earnhardt Miller and everyone in our pits cheering, and I have images but no audio to go with it. But that's what makes it so special.

We live in a world today where everything is so premeditated. Every media news conference is mapped out. Even drivers who crash in the heat of the moment, their PR reps usually get to them to polish them up just enough before going on camera.

But that moment on the team radio between Dale and me, there was no one in the world but us, and we were talking as if no one else were listening. We knew it was truly a career-defining win because it was the Daytona 500.

This was the moment that it felt like we answered all the questions about how my final season would go with Dale. We had to prove we could win, so we did it in our first opportunity and in the biggest race of the season.

We were a band of brothers who formed garage bonds that were just as tight away from the track. That's interior mechanic Adam Jordan (on Dale's left) and lead engineer Kevin Meendering celebrating with driver and crew chief. **Credit: Letarte Family Collection**

CHAPTER XII

Math Doesn't Lie, Kids

BEYOND BEING SUCH A FEEL-GOOD story for Dale and the team, the beauty of winning the Daytona 500 was that we left feeling very accomplished. It didn't matter what else happened—all the questions of this being a useless, pointless season were answered.

It was similar to the 2013 playoffs, when the engine blew at Chicagoland. It took the pressure off, and that was why we ran so well.

We went to Phoenix extremely unprepared and hungover, and we finished third in one of the best chess matches I can recall. I was doing the best work I ever had done.

I still find myself second-guessing it now. How good could I have been now as a crew chief with fast cars and calling strategy?

After Phoenix, we nearly won at Las Vegas Motor Speedway. I gambled because we already had a win, and we ran out of gas while leading on the last lap, losing to Brad Keselowski, who had been pushing the pace under the guidance of crew chief Paul Wolfe because they knew we were light on fuel.

I actually turned that Vegas finish into a real-world math problem at my son's school. We showed the video clip from that race to the fifth-grade class, and I taught them how to figure out the fuel mileage with all the calculations. "If fuel weighs this much, and we put this much in, and we have to run these many laps, how far can we go?"

So we showed them the Las Vegas pit stop and then showed me on the pit box as the car left the pits, and we paused the video. I said, "Okay, figure out the calculations! Do we have enough fuel?" I loved watching these fifth-graders do the math to get the answer.

"Okay, did everyone get an answer?"

"Yes, Mr. Letarte, but I must have done my math wrong. You said the race was 267 laps, but I get 266.3 laps of fuel."

"No, you didn't do your math wrong."

And then we'd hit Play, and I said, "Math doesn't lie, kids. We ran out of gas at 266.3 laps right there." And they loved it, because it was a real-world application.

So we ran out of gas at Vegas, but we would have won otherwise. And then everyone forgot that we nearly were victorious at Darlington Raceway. Kevin Harvick dominated the race, but a pit call put us in the lead for the completion of the race's scheduled distance.

It took two green-white-checkered finishes in overtime for Harvick to pass us for the win. One fewer caution, and we would have won the Southern 500.

We were on a tear at this point.

At Talladega, Dale had the best car just like at Daytona, led twenty-six laps, and was in front with thirty-seven to go. We pitted to make the finish, and Dale restarted eighth. He had to lift while changing lanes a couple of laps later, and he fell out of the lead draft.

And then he stopped trying, riding in the pack until the end of the race without trying to claw his way back to the front.

Dale finished twenty-sixth, and his fan base was so upset, he taped a special edition of his podcast that week to apologize.

I was so angry. That was the one track I never won at with Dale that I really wanted to win. He was the pied piper there, and they would have torn those stands down if he'd won.

I had won at Talladega many times with Jeff Gordon's team, and Dale had won six times at Talladega without me. We both had trophies stacked up there, but none with each other.

* * * * *

But we hit our stride again during the summer by sweeping the races at Pocono Raceway. The first win was the reverse of Vegas, as Brad Keselowski essentially handed us the victory. We were faster than him, but I don't think we could have passed him.

But with five laps to go, even though he already was locked into the playoffs with a victory, he tried to maneuver behind a lapped car to get trash off his front grille to keep his engine from overheating. Who cared if he blew up? He already had a win.

We certainly didn't care, and Dale took the opportunity to pass him for the win.

Win two of the 2014 season at Pocono Raceway.
Credit: Letarte Family Collection

I felt a little guiltier about how we won the second race at Pocono because we beat our teammate Jeff Gordon and crew chief Alan Gustafson on a pure strategy play.

The media didn't fully grasp how I'd been able to do it, because it was a little more detailed tactically than usual, one step beyond the normal pit strategy.

A caution came out, and there was no way to reach the finish; everyone was about eight laps short on fuel. We had all the metric run to where we had to restart, which was inside the top eight. We pitted and took four tires and filled up on fuel, and everyone thought we were idiots when we restarted sixth.

I told Dale on the radio, "All right, I'm going to see you again real soon, and you've got to go on this restart."

He thought he understood why. "Yeah, yeah, yeah. I got it."

"No, listen to me very carefully," I told him. "The next five laps are going to determine the winner. Do you understand what I'm telling you? I need you to restart as if it's a green-white-checkered finish."

"Got it."

They dropped the green, and Dale drove into turn 1 as if it were for the win, even though there still were more than thirty laps to go. He was three wide and chopping off other guys' lanes. And it was because he had to be close enough to Gordon. If we get stuck in traffic and he built a gap, we were done.

Because I knew I needed four seconds' worth of fuel. I knew Gordon still needed to stop for four tires and a thirteen-second pit stop. So there was a nine-second delta between our stop and Gordon's. I'd run the metrics on every race at Pocono to understand on the average what position was nine seconds behind the leader on every lap after the restart.

So we had this figured out, and we actually pitted a lap early because we were losing time to the lead because of traffic. If we ran one more lap, we wouldn't pass Gordon. We were losing time.

I pulled my engineers aside and said, "Listen, don't pay attention to anything except when we reach this gap between us and Gordon. Hit me when you see it. I don't care if you punch me. We have to pit on the next lap."

So with a lap before we thought we could make the stop, my engineer started hitting me, and I radioed Dale. "Come this time! Come this time!"

He pitted, we filled up with fuel, and that was when the TV broadcast caught me making a funny face and a gloating head shake as I made a note in my book on the box.

We had won the race basically with Formula 1–level math. Can you do it on two stops or three? We did it in a way that others hadn't considered and outsmarted them.

This was a testament to how good my working relationship was with the other key members of the team. Kevin Meendering handled the setup. I spent time on pit strategy, more than any other crew chief in the garage, because I was able to delegate so much to the engineers. It was almost unfair how well we all balanced one another's workload.

I consider Alan Gustafson the most underrated crew chief in the pits—he has an engineering degree and is way smarter than I am—and that day, I was able to beat him purely by being more creative.

Break out the broom: Dale and I were the first team to sweep a season at Pocono since 2006. **Credit: Letarte Family Collection**

* * * * *

Another highlight of the summer was at Sonoma Raceway, a road course where Dale had usually struggled.

The Daytona 500 victory meant a lot, but we had finished second in that race twice already.

Before 2014, Dale never had finished in the top ten at Sonoma. Ever.

We weren't even close.

Every year we would test the road courses to try to improve, but in our last year, I said, "Nope." We didn't even build a new car. I think we were the only car in the top thirty that didn't test on a road course. We went in cold turkey.

This was a new attitude that we had from winning Daytona. There was zero pressure because we already were in the playoffs. It wasn't like we weren't trying, but we could race like it didn't matter how we finished.

It was a different approach from how I'd run the team in the past. I like hiring people who work like their jobs are on the line even when they aren't. They don't ever fall into a comfortable environment.

While that sounds like a good thing, what the 2014 season showed was perhaps it sometimes worked against us.

I treated every day at Hendrick as if it were a job interview and someone wanted my position—because someone always does.

But what I learned in 2014 was how to maintain that drive with a new level of comfort. We were going to treat every day as if our jobs depended on it, but we weren't going to get hung up on the results.

So we decided that we weren't going to test Sonoma even though we'd finished forty-first, twenty-third, and twelfth the past three years. We had always tested in the past, because what would you tell Rick Hendrick, who was raising all this money for you to go fast? "Oh, you just don't want to go? You're too busy? You're too tired?"

This year, I just said, "Nope. We're not testing." I remember Chad Knaus being stunned by my decision. But here's how I looked at it.

I love Dale, and for thirty-four of the thirty-six races every year, it's probably at least an even split between what matters more, car or driver. Sometimes the car is even more important because he can drive only to the limits of what's available.

But for two races a year, Sonoma and Watkins Glen, Dale was the weak link—and more so at Sonoma—because he believed that, and it made him an even weaker link.

To use another golf analogy, it was like teeing off on a hole, and if you look at the fairway, you hit it there every time. But if you look at the water, that's where it's going.

Dale would stare at Sonoma and drive it right into the ground. He would get anxiety about the track the minute we began testing there.

I decided to just believe in him as a driver. We wouldn't build a new car. We wouldn't set expectations. *You can't win there, so it doesn't matter.*

If we didn't have to go, we would have stayed at home.

But we did have to go. So we made it a good time.

We went out and enjoyed the Bay Area. We hung out at Petaluma. We drank beer. We just relaxed and had zero expectations. We just had a good time—Dale, spotter T.J. Majors, their significant others, and I as the fifth wheel.

But we still prepared for the race. I told him, "Here's the deal, every time I put you on the right strategy on a road course, you play defense. We get run into the gravel. It doesn't work. This time, people are going to laugh at my strategy, and you need to stick with me."

On Friday of Sonoma weekend, we didn't even make qualifying laps. Dale hadn't been on a road course in nearly a year, so I told him, "Just give us ten laps, and let's see where we're at."

The rest of the teams in the garage thought we were crazy. Everyone was making one- and two-lap qualifying runs, and we were experimenting with several packages like we would in a test session when we had hours to try things instead of ninety minutes. Crews were thrashing all around us, and we just enjoyed ourselves.

Dale still qualified well—seventeenth, his best starting spot in six years. And then on Saturday, I explained my unconventional strategy. I wanted Dale to know that I was going to look like a dummy by bringing him in constantly for tires, which were beginning to matter as wear became a factor at Sonoma and Goodyear employed a softer tire.

Double-file restarts the last few years also had changed the game. It used to be that with twenty laps remaining, you pitted a last time, and the crew chief could head to the airport. He wasn't going to be a factor.

But with double-file restarts, now if you were starting twentieth, you were in the tenth row instead of twentieth in line, with no hope of gaining more than five spots. If you had fresh tires from the tenth row, you could gain eight spots just buzzing up the hill through the esses.

This is what makes pit strategies so hard. It's like trying to bet on the stock market. The variables always are changing.

On road courses, the goal normally is to limit yourself to two to three pit stops. Carl Edwards still won the race in 2014 on a two-stop strategy. That still is the race strategy if you have a winning car.

But what I discovered is, if you have a solid car and don't pretend you're a race winner, you can make tires work for you.

It's kind of like Dale at Daytona—everybody there has to have tires, but my man is so good he just needs track position. He doesn't care if his car drives poorly, because he can overcome that on his own.

At Sonoma, I told Dale, "We're just going to keep pitting." I could see him understand it and also knew that if it didn't work, then, buddy, we would just blame my pit strategy. I'd stand up in front of everybody and say, "Man, we tried it, and it didn't work."

We pitted five times in our final race at Sonoma—two times more than anyone else in the race. I ran out of tires because I just kept putting them on. The second-to-last caution came with twenty-five laps remaining, he pitted, and everyone else behind him came too.

I told him, "You think you suck here, but you're on better tires than everyone in front of you. We're done pitting now, and we're going forward from here." And he got it. There was no complaining from him.

Dale charged from eleventh to a career-best Sonoma finish of third over the final twenty-five laps. If the race had been two laps longer, he would have won.

The fact that I wasn't justifying my job or trying to keep my job forced me to come up with the best strategy and approach and plan.

Sometimes the solution to a problem is unconventional. Sometimes history doesn't tell you the best way. Sometimes you have to look between the lines of history.

Before that season, every crew chief (including me) prepared to approach Sonoma with Dale the same way. It took years of notes and stats, the impending departure from my job, and the Daytona 500 victory to approach it a different way.

The unconventional worked. Other than winning the Daytona 500, that was probably our biggest race of 2014.

A photographer caught the family selfie in progress.
Credit: Letarte Family Collection

CHAPTER XIII

The Longest Walk of My Career

IF SONOMA, TWO WINS AT Pocono, and the Daytona 500 triumph were among the absolute peaks of the season, the valley had to have been Kansas Speedway, the opener to the second round of the playoffs.

The 2014 season was the first of a new playoff structure with elimination rounds and an expansion of the field from twelve to sixteen teams. Four teams would be eliminated after the round of sixteen, which would consist of three races—Chicagoland, New Hampshire, and Dover.

We hardly put any effort in the first-round races because we knew being one of the twelve to advance would be easy.

We put every effort into Kansas because we knew we could do well on a repaved track. We kicked everyone's asses at both Pocono races. We kicked their asses at Michigan. Just like those tracks, this was a race on a similarly repaved surface.

Not to mention, Kansas was the track where Dale had suffered a concussion in a 2012 testing crash that led to him missing two races a couple of months later. In 2011, we had beaten all but one car at Kansas (finishing behind Brad Keselowski's fuel mileage gamble).

I had a bone to pick with this place, and we had extra motivation that it would be even sweeter to lay to rest all those memories with a victory that advanced us into the third round of our championship quest.

We were going to fly there.

The weekend went smoothly. Dale qualified eighth and practiced well. The race started simple and went according to plan. We used strategy to take the lead on a lap 91 restart, and I was coaching him to avoid pushing too hard.

"There's no reason to get carried away."

Dale easily led for thirty-two laps. And then his right-front tire exploded while he was running at about 70 percent.

Boom. I was watching off turn 4 as Dale pounded the fence.

"I wasn't even trying hard, Stevie. I was trying to go slow."

We had put all our eggs in the Kansas basket to advance to the next round. We weren't very good at Charlotte, and Talladega was too much of a lottery to count on despite how good Dale was there.

So Kansas was circled on our calendar.

And our plan worked perfectly from the time we built the car all the way until it hit the wall on lap 123.

Next to the moment at Phoenix in 2007, when I lost the championship as Jeff Gordon's crew chief, Kansas was the only other race in my career that I wish I could redo, because that cost us the championship.

This was one of the two loneliest walks I ever had in motorsports. The first was from the pit box to the Phoenix garage in 2007, because I knew I'd be facing a Jeff Gordon who had lost a shot at winning his fifth championship.

And the other was from the pit box at Kansas to the garage in 2014 to see if we could fix Dale's car while knowing we had lost any shot of winning a championship together in our last season.

The 2007 season was disheartening because we gave it our absolute best and we just flat got beat by a better team in Jimmie Johnson and Chad Knaus.

But this time, we executed the plan perfectly and just fell to misfortune while Dale was barely pushing the car. I'm not putting the blame on Goodyear. It's possible we ran over some debris.

But it was demoralizing.

We were in our rhythm and had the race won.

It was like that movie *The Matrix*, watching in slow motion as Dale hit the wall. Was that really our car?

All the anxiety or reservations I had about leaving crew-chiefing were gone.

The disappointment of 2007 crushed me but also inspired me to do many more things. The Kansas crash in 2014 had the opposite effect; it was a reminder of why some days, the job wasn't worth it.

Another disappointing crash for us at Kansas Speedway, where Dale was running about 70 percent when his tire popped. **Credit: Harold Hinson Photography**

I was done. I couldn't do this anymore. I knew I was ready to do TV.

Kansas sufficiently took the wind out of our sails for Charlotte, where we struggled to a twentieth-place finish as expected.

At Talladega, Dale ran well and led thirty-one laps around the race's midpoint, but he got shuffled back in the middle groove and never regained the lost positions in traffic. He placed thirty-first after getting pushed into a crash during a green-white-checkered finish.

Dale is more successful at Talladega than anybody. But if you're counting on that track for anything, you are already grasping at straws, because so much of it is out of your control. It's like trying to control the weather.

We knew we were sunk when we hit the wall at Kansas. It was like a fighter taking a heavy shot in the eighth round but finally getting knocked out in the eleventh. That right hook three rounds earlier was what changed all of it.

We were leaving Talladega, officially out of the playoffs, and the mood instantly shifted from focusing on the championship to savoring our final four races together.

* * * * *

Dale and I didn't say it, but it was a conversation we didn't need to have. It became clear the end was in sight, and we entered Martinsville knowing damn well we were going to enjoy those last four races.

We were starting in the right place for it, because Martinsville meant a lot to Dale as the one track he wanted to conquer, and it held so many important memories for both of us.

On October 23, 2005, I'd won my first race as a crew chief there with Jeff Gordon. On April 3, 2011, Dale and I nearly had won for the first time as a duo together before being passed in the closing laps there by Kevin Harvick. In 2012, Dale returned from a concussion there, and it led to a teachable moment for both of us about setting expectations.

We were rolling back into this little paper clip–shaped half-mile just over the North Carolina border in Virginia, where so much had happened.

Much like Daytona, there were no dreams of winning at Martinsville—we were just going to have a damn fun time. There was nothing about the weekend that stood out about our car in practice or qualifying (Dale started twenty-third, the lowest qualifier of a winner there in twelve years).

There was no magical sign or shining light that it was going to be a great weekend—until a few yellow flags in the final eighty laps played into our hands.

We won Martinsville when a caution with six laps remaining synched with our strategy. I put fresh tires on the car, and Dale took the lead from Tony Stewart and led the final four laps.

I remember very clearly that Dale stood on the gas when he got inside of Stewart in turns 3 and 4, sending the message that it was his race to win. *Either get out of the way or I'll move you out of the way with these fresh tires.*

It caused a flashback to 2011, when Dale overdrove the corner and allowed Kevin Harvick to beat us without having to touch us. This is what experience does for you. Dale knew how to win it this time.

There was some urgency at the end too. Jeff Gordon, who still was alive in the playoffs, was coming hard toward the front, and I remember thinking in the back of my mind that it would mean way more to him than us to win and advance to the final round.

But Dale wasn't letting this one go. After he passed Stewart, it was all about just putting together six more perfect corners. This was after running 750 or so laps over the course of the weekend. It was all about not making more of it than it was.

Brake. Curb. Turn. Off the brake. Gas. Straightaway.

Five more times.

Early in our career, Dale and I sat down and figured out where he struggled the most. "Man, I suck at Darlington. I suck at Fontana. And Dover."

So we worked at making him better at all those, but I also asked him where he wanted to win.

He got a gleam in his eye, and he said, "I'm just an old short-track racer. There is nothing ——ing cooler than Martinsville."

I used to bust on him because I'd won there so many times with Jeff. That was where we won our first race together in October 2005.

Dale would talk about how special Martinsville was and how he wanted to win there, and I'd interrupt him and say, "Whoa, whoa. I want to win there *again*. I've got a grandfather clock in my house."

After the win, I said I hoped to be having a cold beer with Dale at his house ten years later, and *his* clock would chime, and we'd smile.

Martinsville -- the track where Dale always had wanted
to win – was our final victory lane appearance together.
Credit: Letarte Family Collection

At Dale's house, that clock is in his foyer. You walk in, and there's a table and that clock. And he has his Daytona 500 trophies, both of them just sitting there in his living room. That's what I love about him.

That was why that victory at Martinsville was so special. We were resigned to the fact that we probably weren't going to win again in our final four races together. We were ready to tear that place down celebrating when we did.

It also was a special weekend for me because I had my daughter, Ashlyn, with me by myself. She and Doug Yates's twins slept over in my bus Saturday night. (Papa Bear, as they call me, was in charge of all three girls.)

Doug was heading back with his family about halfway through the race Sunday, and Ashlyn was planning to return with them until she was encouraged to stay under Motor Racing Outreach ministry supervision and go home with me.

After the win, MRO brought Ashlyn to victory lane, and it was spectacular. I have a photo from there with Ashlyn, Dale, and Amy. Then I brought her to the media center with me for interviews. We even made her a placard for the postrace news conference.

While Dale had Amy to celebrate at Martinsville, Ashlyn was the sole representative for the Letarte family. **Credit: Letarte Family Collection**

After the win, I dropped my little girl off at home, and then I went to Dale's house, and we partied in his basement until the sun came up. We jumped on a golf cart and rode around his property.

In your career, rarely do you get to enjoy a victory as we did that one. Even after our winning Daytona, it immediately was on to Phoenix and the next race.

With three races left together, we celebrated this win as if it were our last, because we knew it could be.

And it wasn't just me leaving. At least half the team would move on after 2014, and I think Dale wanted to win one more time with that group.

In his first Cup ride at Dale Earnhardt Inc., Dale also had a really close-knit team of good friends and family members. Our team was the same way, and we also had been a part of his career resurgence. We made the playoffs every year. We won five races, including the Daytona 500 and my favorite short track.

We definitely were a standout group of the teams he had worked with in his career.

CHAPTER XIV

A Normal Life

MY FINAL RACE WITH THE team at Homestead-Miami Speedway was one of the toughest of my life because I didn't know what to expect.

Dale organized a goodbye dinner Friday night—which is notable because Dale usually doesn't organize anything. We went to a seafood restaurant, and they gave me an old-fashioned popcorn machine, because I saw one at a restaurant earlier in the year while we were out in Dover.

"Man, that's badass," I said then. "I'd love to have one."

We had this whole conversation about it at dinner, and then I forgot about it. That was what they surprised me with as a going-away present. It's in my basement now, and I still use it to make popcorn.

Dale also had an artist do a sketch of the team off a still photo of all of us. When I saw that, it drove home that this was about more than one guy leaving a race team. We were more than that, and those thoughts were what made the rest of the weekend difficult at the track.

I was being followed by a crew from NBC Sports to document all the "last" times we were doing something together, from the practices to qualifying to the team debriefings. I was torn about whether we should have the cameras there, because I wasn't sure about the distractions and how I would handle my emotions.

Also concerning was whether it would slight Dale, but he handled it all well.

It also was a special weekend for my family, who was interviewed by the TV crew Saturday afternoon. My daughter said she was excited to have Daddy home more often so we could walk to get doughnuts. On the night before the race, we had a celebration dinner with our family and friends, and Tricia and the kids baked a cake for me.

Having them there through this just reaffirmed that my decision to leave the pit box was the correct one.

I was doing well through practice and qualifying, and then at the start of the race, I stuck my head in the car to talk to Dale, and I started crying like a baby.

He laughed back at me and said something that helped me regain my composure. I'd love to tell you what it was, but in that moment, full of emotion, I have no idea what his words really were.

Then I took my final walk from the car to my pit box as I had at the beginning of every race in my crew chief career. I high-fived all my guys and climbed atop the box for the start of the race.

Then Rick Hendrick came on the radio, and I lost it again.

I can't even recall everything he said, but basically, it was like, "These twenty years with you have been great. We wish you weren't leaving. We love you."

That was tough. And then when the race started, I was able to settle into it, even though it wasn't that memorable. Dale finished fourteenth, and afterward, I gathered my wife and son, Tyler, who watched the race sitting behind me, and we took a photo on top of the pit box.

Family portrait before I climbed off the pit box for the final time as a Cup crew chief. **Credit: Letarte Family Collection**

* * * * *

And then it just was weird for a while.

I came back from Florida, and I cleaned out my office to make room for Greg Ives, the new crew chief. I left a win sticker for him on my keyboard, like presidents who leave an Oval Office letter for their successors. It was my way of saying "This is what this office was built upon."

Then there was the awards ceremony in Las Vegas, which allowed me to celebrate a final time with Dale (where our relationship had started with him in earnest four years earlier).

When we returned home, it took a while to accept the new rhythm of my life after two decades in racing.

I purposefully pulled away from it and didn't reach out to people I knew. I didn't want to infringe on Greg settling into his new role.

And then it all made sense on May 3, 2015, when I was taking Tyler to a flag football game on a Sunday afternoon in South Charlotte. I had the race on my radio while driving, and Dale was leading, and it took me back to the conversations we had, particularly the one late in 2013 about my departure.

One thing he always said was that I was responsible for helping ensure the team would be in a good place after my exit.

"You've got to get the replacement," Dale told me. "You've got to help me get somebody good. You're in charge of it. You know the guys. You know what I need. Get my guy!"

I actually didn't have much input. Greg was Rick Hendrick's choice, and I didn't disagree with it. The team actually didn't ask my opinion, but I think Greg was a good choice regardless.

He was at JR Motorsports, winning the Xfinity championship with Chase Elliott, after he had been the engineer with Chad Knaus for Jimmie Johnson's first five championships. I helped convince Greg to take that crew chief job at JRM, which was Dale's team, as several Hendrick employees moved into that organization.

And while I loved all the crew guys on my team, the guy I worried the most about feeling as if I were bailing on him was Dale, because we had a unique relationship.

So I was listening to him dominate the second half of the Talladega race while I drove Ty to his flag football game.

It was vintage Dale. He went to the top. He led when it cut to single file. He controlled the race all the way down to the closing laps. Nobody could mount a charge. He was in command, and I felt like I was a lap ahead of the radio commentators.

I knew what he was doing ahead of every move he made. Though we never won Talladega together, he had told me enough that I knew how he would do it. It felt as if I were listening to a race he had described in his brain one hundred times.

And I was at peace. We pulled into the parking lot, and I sat there listening while Ty went on the football field for warm-ups.

As I watched my kid get ready to play football, I felt like I was listening to another kid graduate from high school as Dale won at Talladega. They were the emotions you might experience as an older brother or someone happy for a best friend. This feeling of "All right!"

He won, and I didn't have any anxiety or ill will. Sure, it would have been nice to have been there, but I was happy, truly happy for him and Greg.

I'm sure it's similar to leaving behind a job that you loved and watching your coworkers thrive in your absence. There are emotions to work through, and you don't know how you'll react to it. Will you be jealous, wishing you still were part of it?

Then at some point, they have success and you are genuinely happy for them. It's a moment in life that something wonderful happens to someone you care about, and there isn't an ounce of resentment, just pure joy that it happened for them.

I was truly happy for Dale and Greg.

I sent him a text, got out of the car, and watched the football game. When I got back in the car, I had a text reply from him. To think I had even a small part in leading the way to the first victory without me made me as proud as I was happy.

Two months later at Daytona, I got to enjoy the same emotions again. In my debut race in the NBC Sports booth, Dale won again (in another rain-delayed race that didn't end until after 2:00 a.m.). I went to victory lane at Daytona to congratulate him.

I didn't get the chance to congratulate him that way after his win at Talladega, but the moment still was perfect.

I left the team by making the decision to have a normal life with my family. And there I was while listening to the race, fighting interstate traffic to take my kid to a flag football game. I was about as normal as I could be.

And I was about as happy too. For him and for me.

EPILOGUE

JUST LIKE REBUILDING A RACE team, I learned that writing a book takes a lot of time and is a much bigger project than I gave it credit.

In the three years since I began working on this story, a lot has happened. When I started writing this book,

- Dale Earnhardt Jr. was winning and contending for a championship;

- Jeff Gordon and Tony Stewart were racing in the Cup Series;

- Jimmie Johnson had won only six championships.

After many cups of coffee, conversations, and rewrites, I now have a book that is being released in a new era of NASCAR:

- Johnson has become a seven-time champion;

- Gordon and Stewart both have retired; and

- my buddy Dale Jr. has gotten married (it was a hell of a party), become a father, and retired from driving to join me in the NBC Sports booth.

Funny enough, as I begin my fourth year of broadcasting in 2018, I'm really excited to be back alongside my old friend and entering a new experience not unlike the one that you've just read about.

I think the lessons we've learned in this book are going to form the cornerstones for the next chapter of a great career together. It's going to make us a great duo together, talking about racing and covering NASCAR for the fans.

I'm sure we'll have a ton of fun and create a bunch of new stories. Maybe enough to fill another book!

—Steve Letarte

Trying to win races at the highest level of motorsports was the best job a guy could want. None of that would have been possible without the love and support of a wonderful family. Tricia, I love you and owe you the world for being the best wife, mother, and sounding board a man could ever ask for. Tyler and Ashlyn, no trophy in the world could ever match how proud I am of you two. You are wonderful kids and will be great in whatever you choose to do in life.

This book talks a lot about Dale and I and our accomplishments. The real truth is none of that ever happens without many, many talented people pulling in the same direction. I will always be indebted to this group. They truly are the secret to any success we were able to have.

STEVE LETARTE IS A NASCAR analyst for NBC Sports Group who spent nine seasons as a crew chief in stock-car racing's premier series. Managing the teams of stars Jeff Gordon and Dale Earnhardt Jr., Letarte called the strategy for fifteen victories (including the 2014 Daytona 500), and his 2007 season with Gordon set a record for most top tens in a season.

A natural leader with a gregarious touch, Letarte also is a motivational speaker and an entrepreneur who founded RacingJobs. com. The Maine native lives in Cornelius, North Carolina, with his wife, Tricia, and their two children, Tyler and Ashlyn.

Nate Ryan is a journalist who has covered NASCAR full-time since 2002, writing for the *Richmond Times-Dispatch*, *USA Today Sports*, and NBC Sports Digital. He also is the host of the NASCAR on NBC podcast and frequent contributor to NASCAR America on NBCSN.